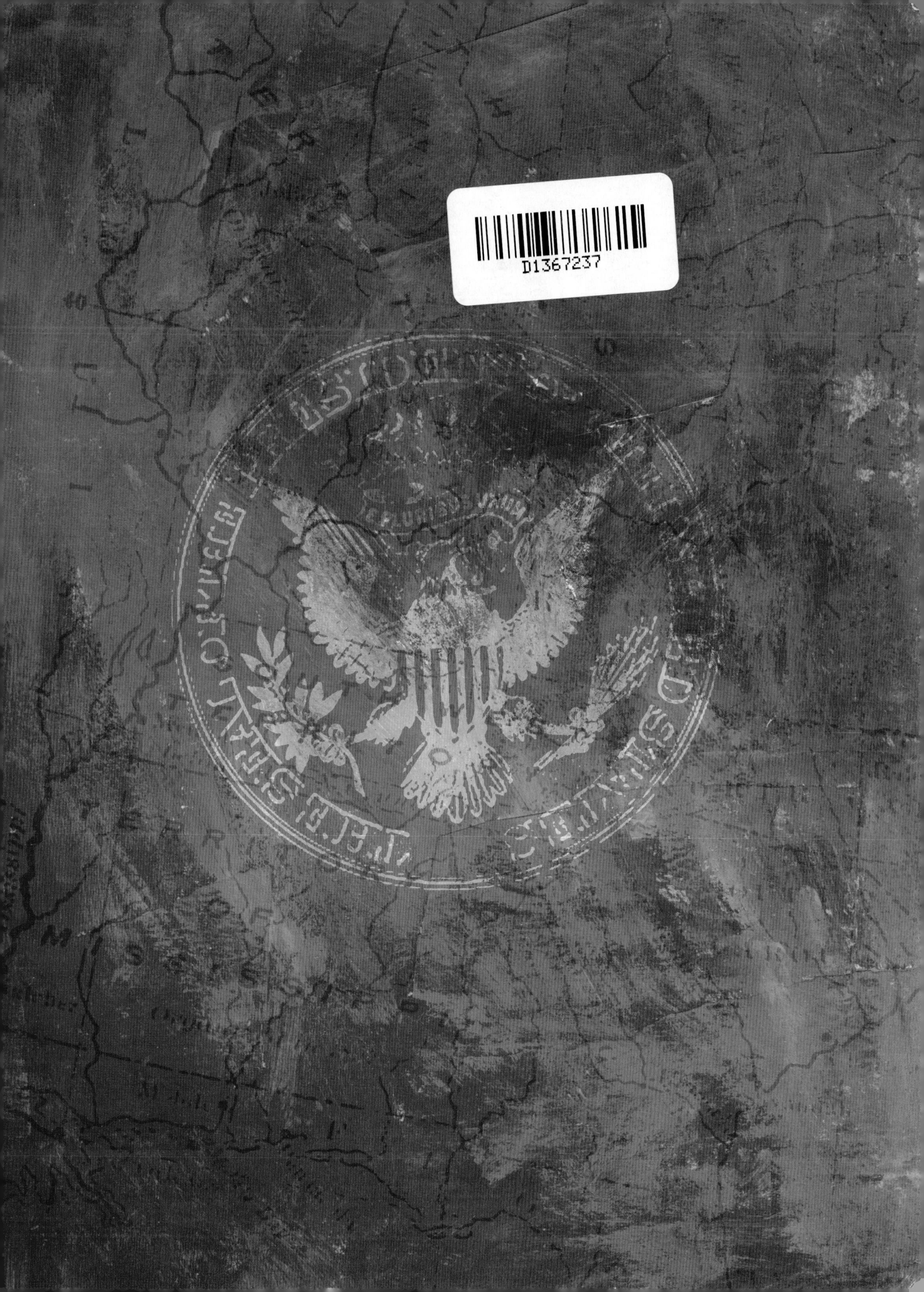
E PLURIBUS UNUM

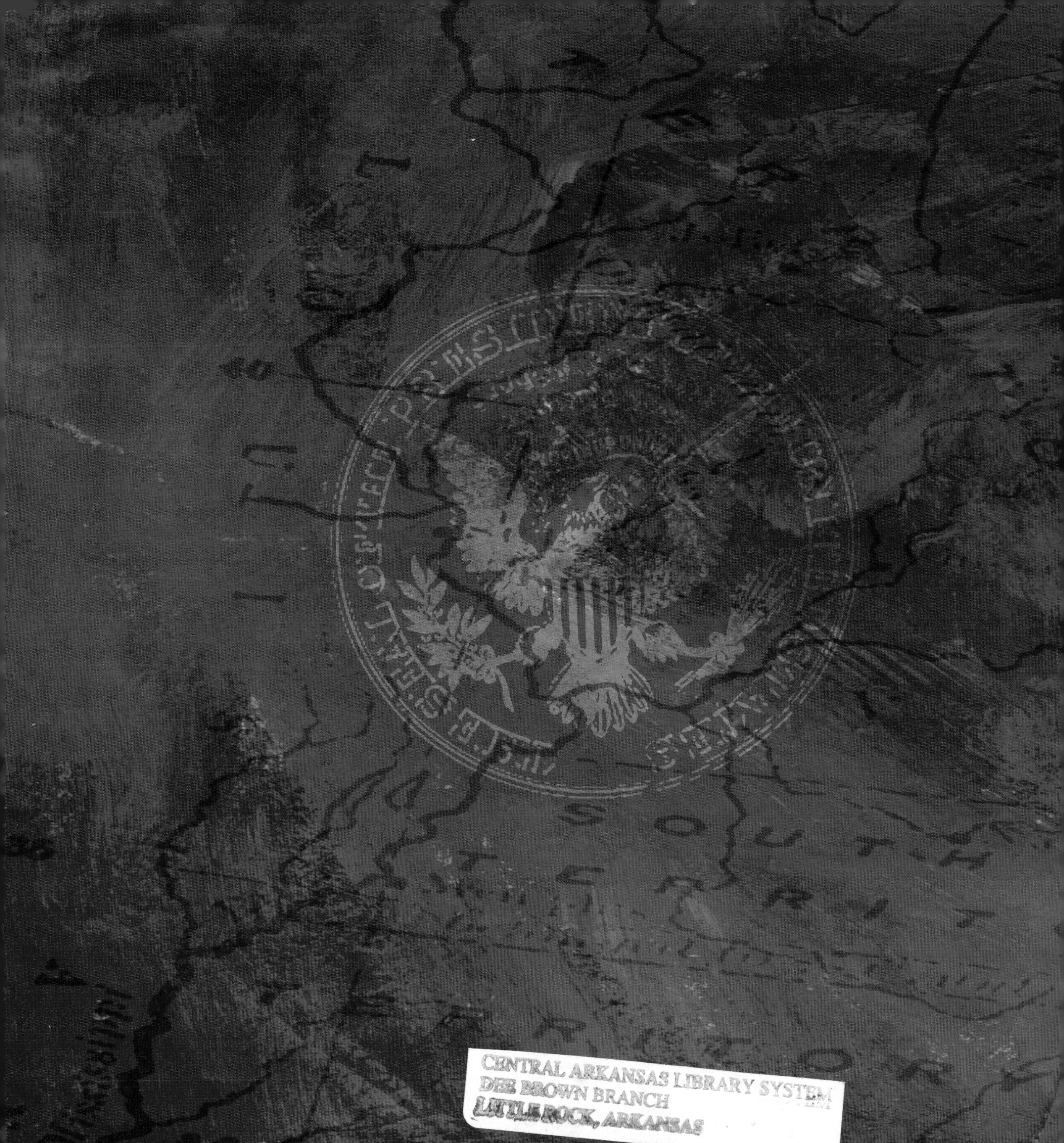

ISBN: 978-1-60010-344-5   12 11 10 09   1 2 3 4   www.idwpublishing.com

Operations: Moshe Berger, Chairman • Ted Adams, Chief Executive Officer • Greg Goldstein, Chief Operating Officer • Matthew Ruzicka, CPA, Chief Financial Officer • Alan Payne, VP of Sales • Lorelei Bunjes, Dir. of Digital Services • Marci Hubbard, Executive Assistant • Alonzo Simon, Shipping Manager • **Editorial:** Chris Ryall, Publisher/Editor-in-Chief • Scott Dunbier, Editor, Special Projects • Andy Schmidt, Senior Editor • Justin Eisinger, Editor • Kris Oprisko, Editor/Foreign Lic. • Denton J. Tipton, Editor • Tom Waltz, Editor • Mariah Huehner, Assistant Editor • **Design:** Robbie Robbins, EVP/Sr. Graphic Artist • Ben Templesmith, Artist/Designer • Neil Uyetake, Art Director • Chris Mowry, Graphic Artist • Amauri Osorio, Graphic Artist

THE PRESIDENTS

OF THE
UNITED STATES

BEN TEMPLESMITH

"You can fool all of the people some of the time, and some of the people all of the time,

but you can not fool all of the people all of the time."

-Abraham Lincoln

George Washington

1st President of the United States (1789-97)

Born: Feb. 22, 1732, Pope's Creek, Va.
Died: Dec. 14, 1799, Mount Vernon, Va.
Profession: Soldier, Planter
Political Affiliation: Federalist

Elected unanimously by the Electoral College in both 1789 and again in the 1792 election.

Declined to be paid salary as president but at the insistence of Congress eventually accepted the then sizable sum of $25,000 a year.

Feared the formation of political parties, believing they would cause conflict and stagnation.

His closest advisors formed two factions, setting the framework for the future First Party System. Secretary of the Treasury Alexander Hamilton had bold plans to establish the national credit and build a financially powerful nation, and formed the basis of the Federalist Party. Secretary of State Thomas Jefferson, founder of the Jeffersonian Republicans, strenuously opposed Hamilton's agenda.

One of only two sitting presidents to take military command in the field, during the Whiskey Rebellion of 1794.

Supported the Jay Treaty where the British agreed to depart their forts around the Great Lakes, the Canadian-U.S. boundary was adjusted, numerous pre-Revolutionary debts were forgiven, and the British opened their West Indies colonies to American trade. Brought about a decade of prosperous trade but angered the French Revolutionary government as America refused to involve itself in the French war against Britain.

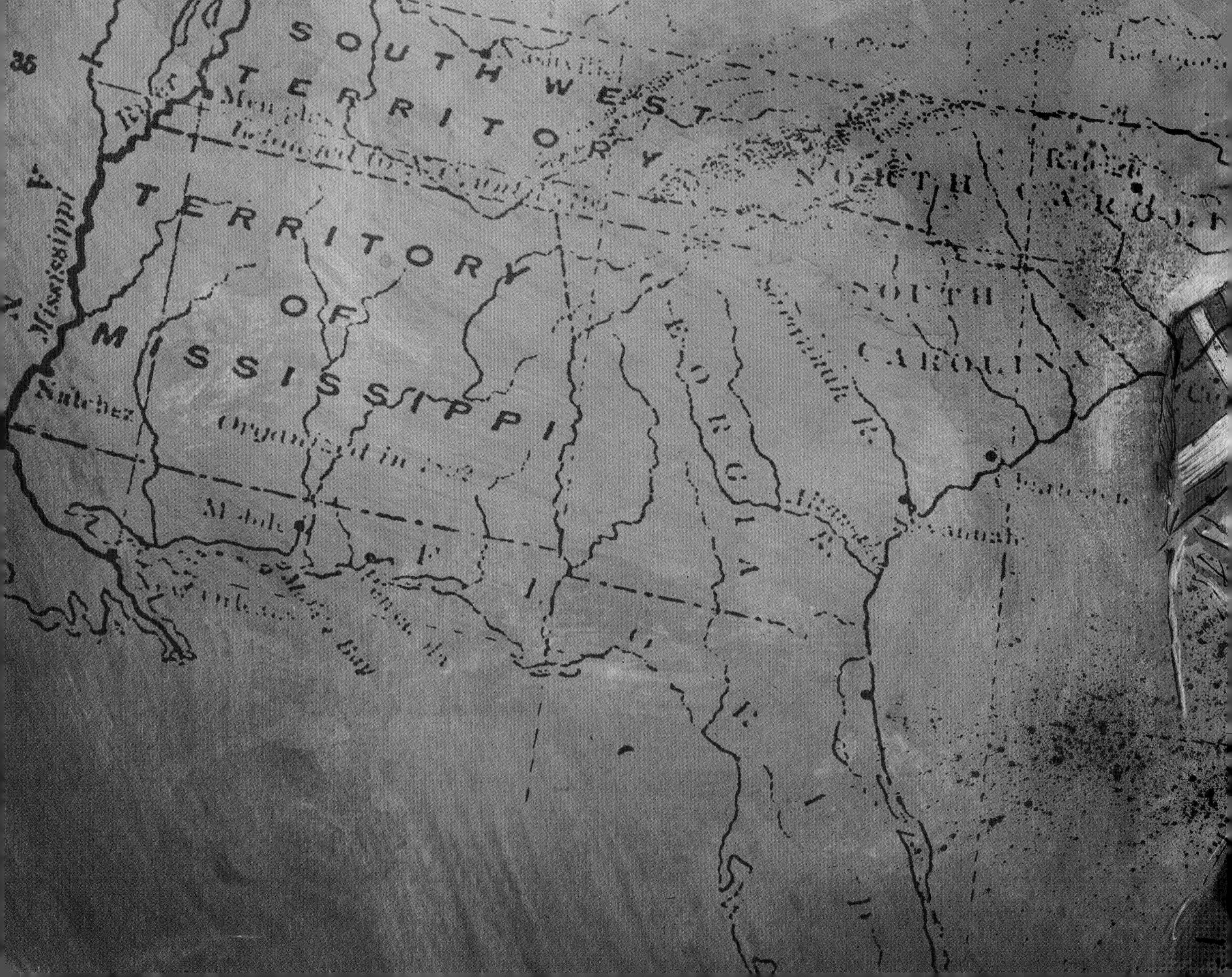
SOUTH WEST TERRITORY
TERRITORY OF MISSISSIPPI
NORTH
SOUTH CAROLINA
Mississippi
Natchez

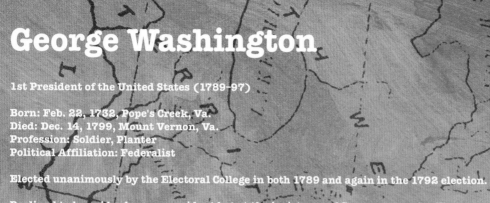

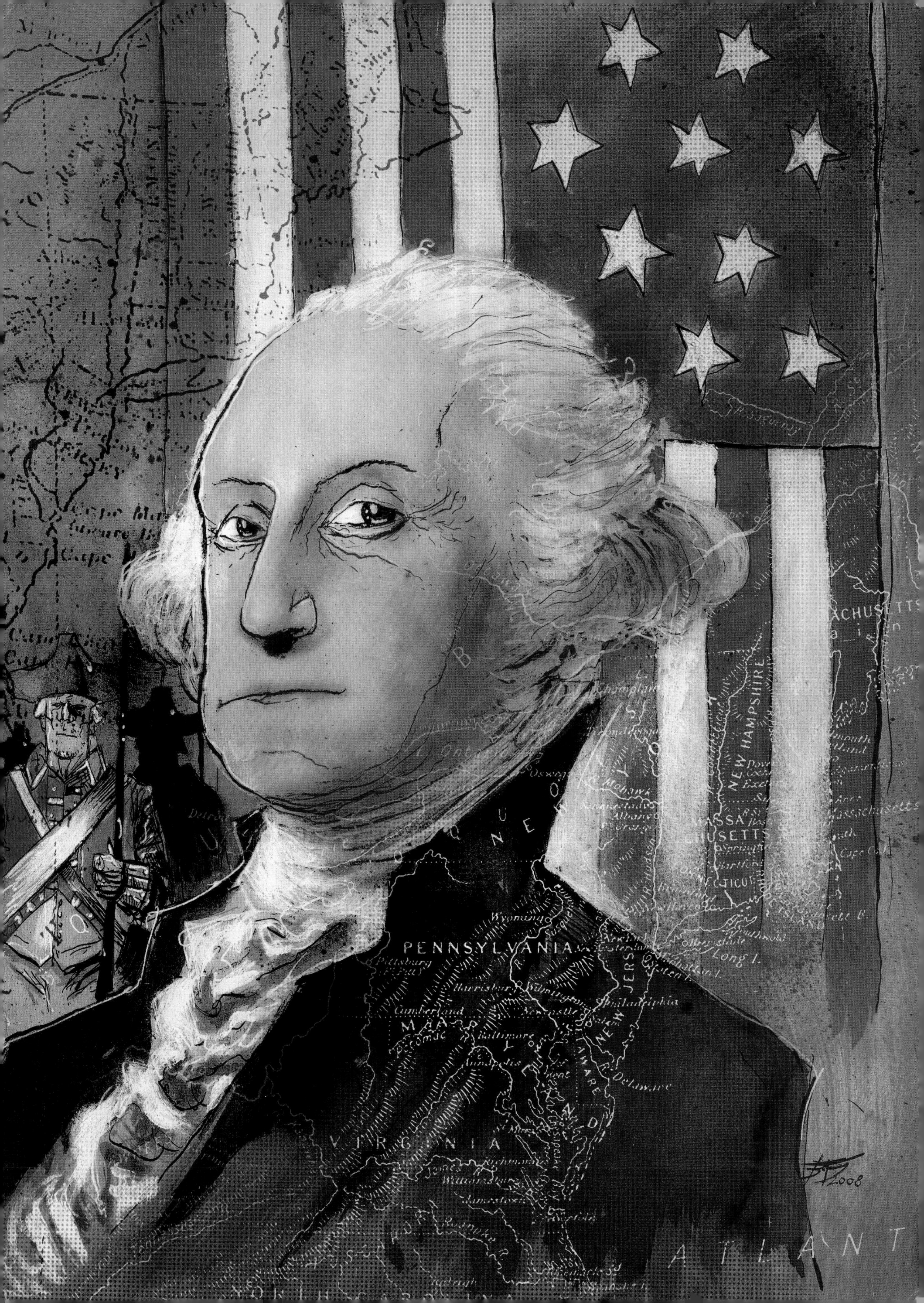
PENNSYLVANIA
VIRGINIA
NEW HAMPSHIRE
Pittsburg
Harrisburg
Philadelphia
Baltimore
Cumberland
Annapolis
Wyoming
Long I.
ATLANT
2008

John Adams

2nd President of the United States (1797–1801)

Born: Oct. 30, 1735, Braintree (now Quincy), Mass.
Died: July 4, 1826, Quincy, Mass.
Profession: Lawyer
Political Affiliation: Federalist

Kept the U.S. out of the French war against Britain, despite France's help in securing American independence. Angered, the French began seizing American merchant ships, resulting in the undeclared naval war known as the "Quasi-war" in 1798 and the augmentation of the U.S. navy.

Signed the Alien and Sedition Acts designed to crack down on political immigrants and domestic Republican opposition. The Sedition Act criminalized anyone who publicly criticized the federal government.

Allowed The Treaty of Alliance of 1778 with France to be superseded, meaning the United States could now be free of foreign entanglements, as Washington had previously advised. Adams avoided war, but deeply split his own Federalist Party in the process.

Just before his 1800 presidential loss, he became the first president to occupy the new, but unfinished President's Mansion on November 1, 1800.

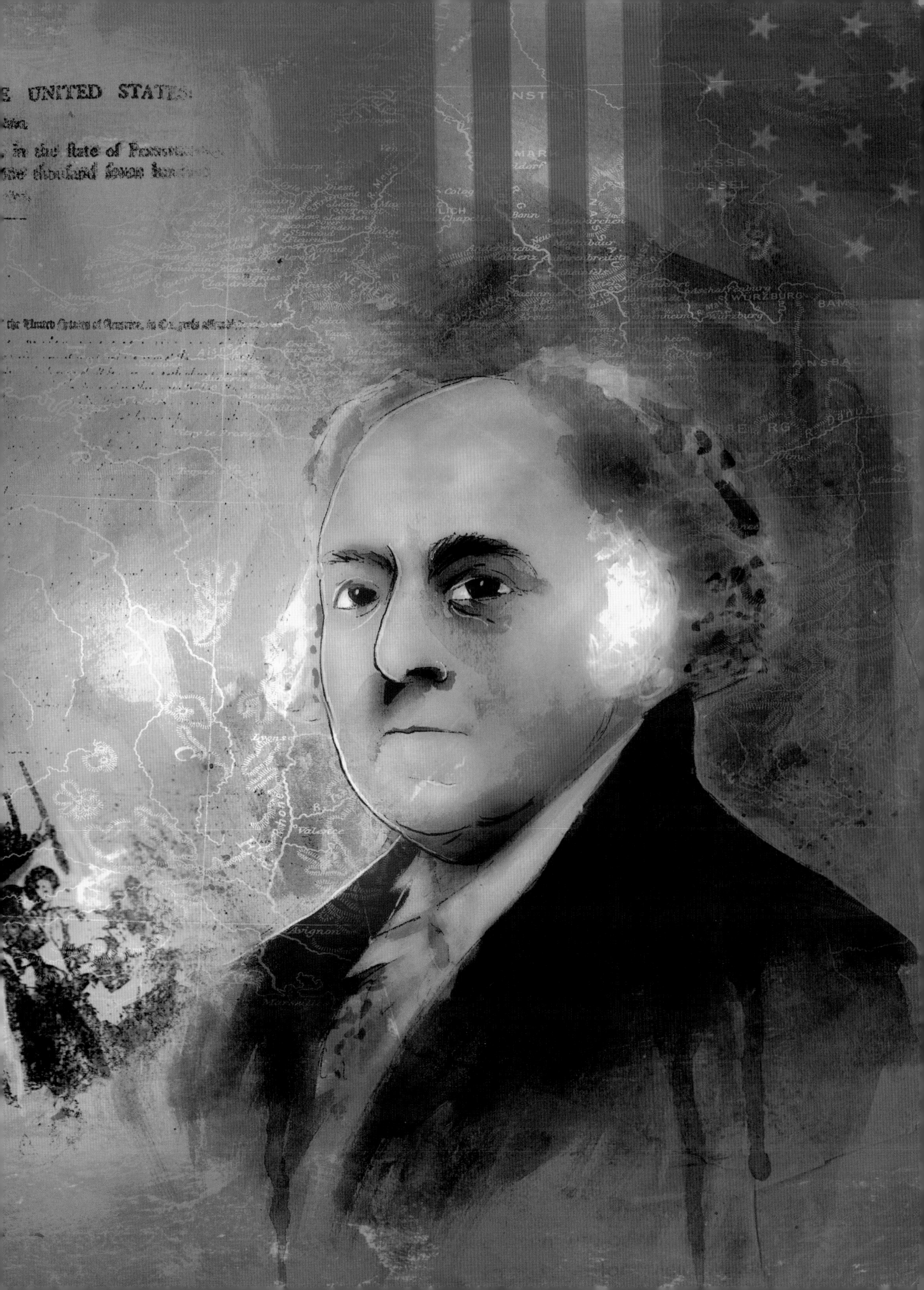

Thomas Jefferson

3rd President of the United States (1801-09)

Born: Apr. 13, 1743, Shadwell plantation, Goochland (now in Albemarle) County, Va.
Died: July 4, 1826, Monticello, near Charlottesville, Va.
Profession: Lawyer, Planter
Political Affiliation: Democratic-Republican

"Jeffersonian Democracy" as it later became known was marked by Jefferson's belief in agrarianism and limited government.

Those imprisoned under the Sedition Acts were released when it expired in 1801.

Attempted to eliminate the national debt. Initially successful but eventually disastrous as the Napoleonic Wars between Britain and France interrupted American trade.

Decreased the size of the U.S. army, believing in the "citizen soldier" but recognizing the need for qualified leadership, created the Army Corps of Engineers, and established the United States Military Academy at West Point in 1802.

Under Jefferson the first Indian relocation began from the southern states.

In 1807, northern representatives in Congress submitted a bill calling for the end of the slave trade. The bill, submitted with Jefferson's approval, divided the Congress along sectional lines. The slave trade was banned but the ban only reduced the trade and did not eliminate it altogether.

Purchased Louisiana from the French, effectively doubling the size of the U.S.

Went to war against the Barbary Pirates, ending in victory by paying a $60,000 ransom for U.S. sailors and signing of a peace treaty with Yussif Karamanli.

Damaged much of his support towards the end of his second presidential term by signing the Embargo Act of 1807, forbidding trade with both Britain and France for not respecting America's neutrality.

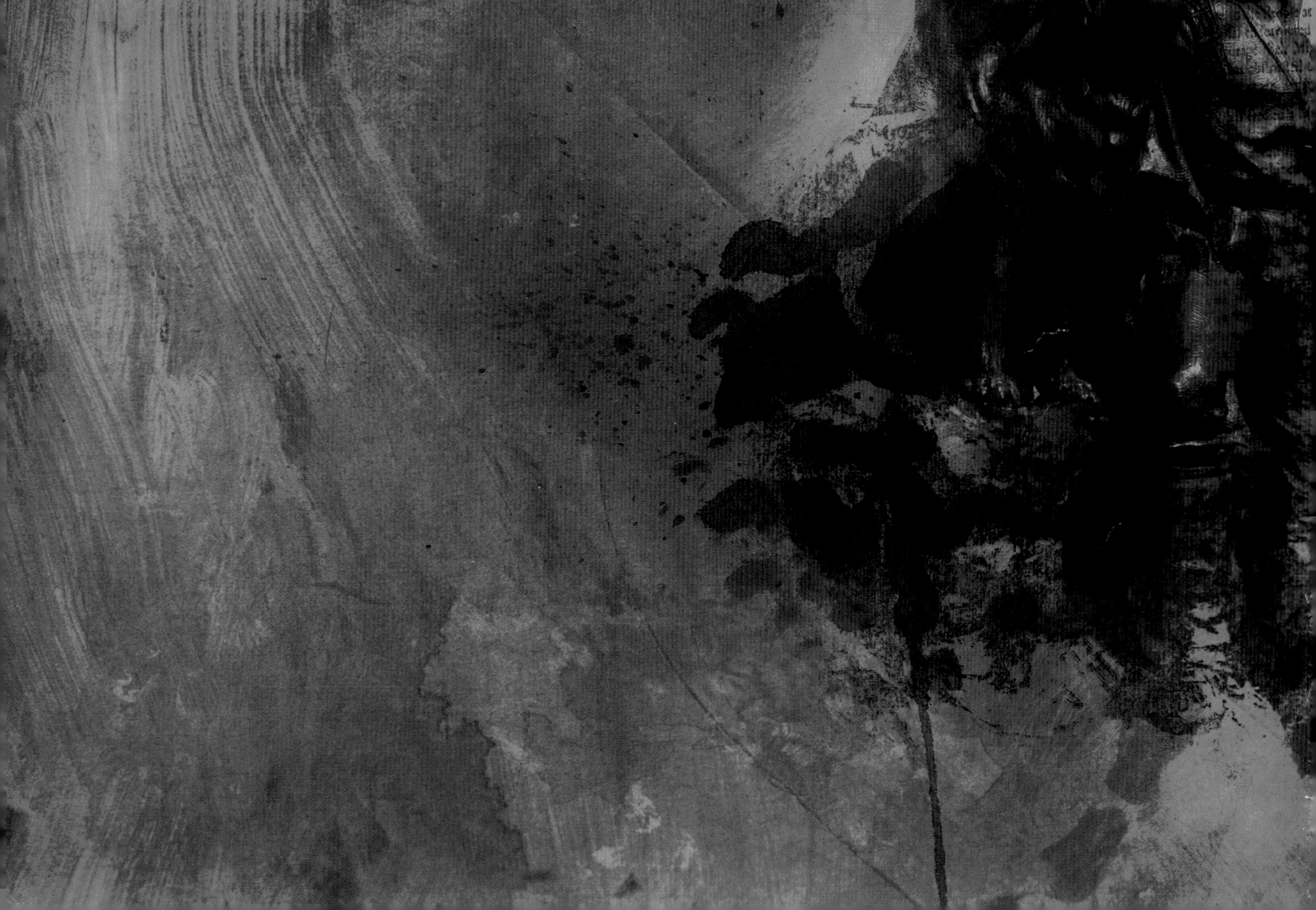

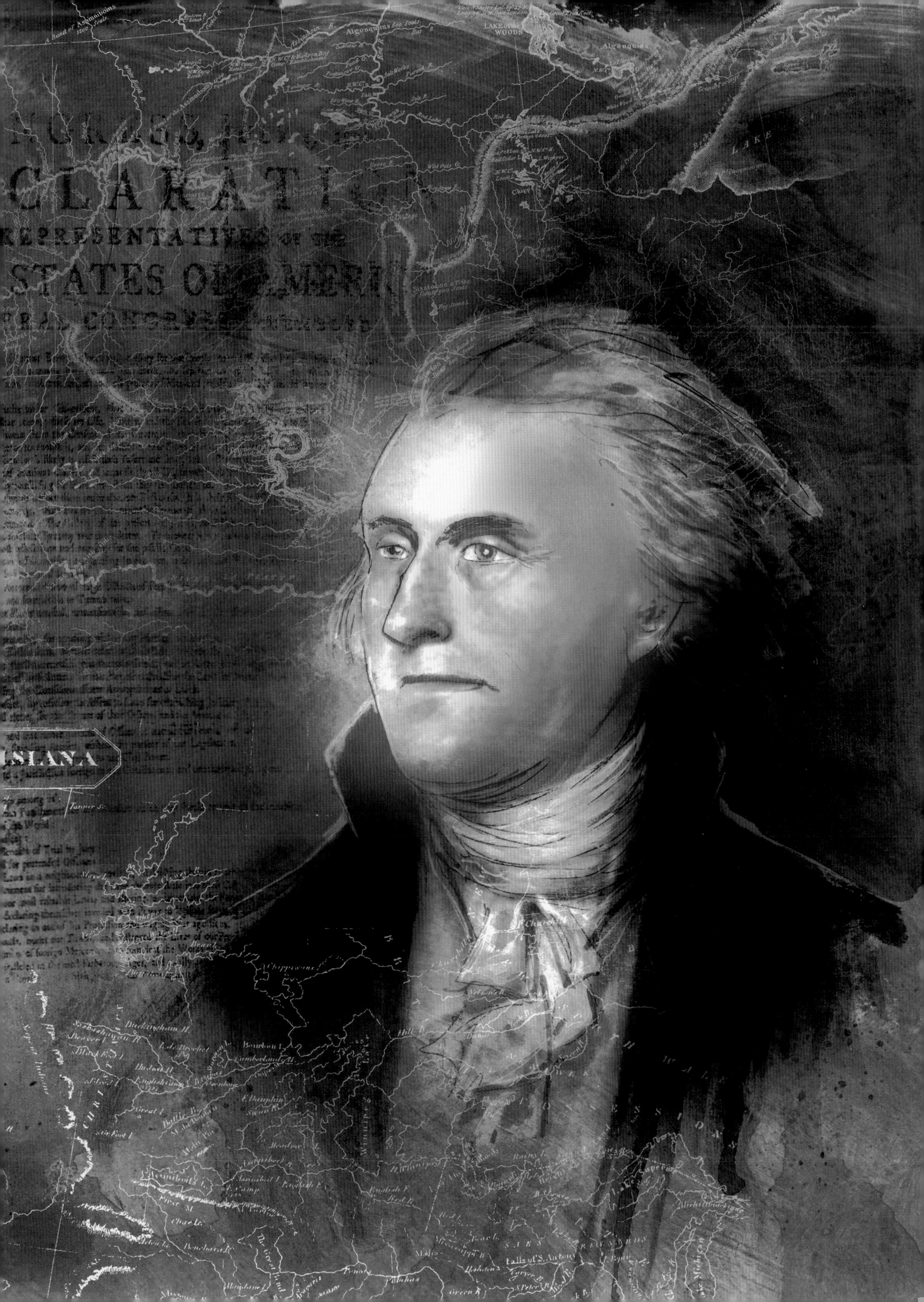
CLARATIO
REPRESENTATIVES OF THE
STATES OF AMERI
LAKE of the WOODS
Algonquins
LSIANA

James Madison

4th President of the United States (1809-17)

Born: Mar. 16, 1751, Port Conway, Va.
Died: June 28, 1836, Monpelier, Va.
Profession: Lawyer
Political Affiliation: Democratic-Republican

Madison convinced Congress to declare war in what was known as the War of 1812 with Britain over its constant seizure of American shipping, and later invaded Canada (British territory).

Britain captured Detroit, occupied Washington D.C., and burned down the first White House as the United States invaded York, Upper Canada (now known as Toronto, Ontario). U.S. naval victory averted an invasion of New York.

War weariness led to the end of conflict after the defeat of Napoleon in 1814. With the causes of war long forgotten, the Treaty of Ghent ended the war in 1815 and the status quo of territories was restored. The United States was swept by a sense of euphoria and national achievement in finally securing solid independence from Britain.

Eventually authorized the Second Bank of the United States after the expiration of the first and hardships of financing with no bank during the war.

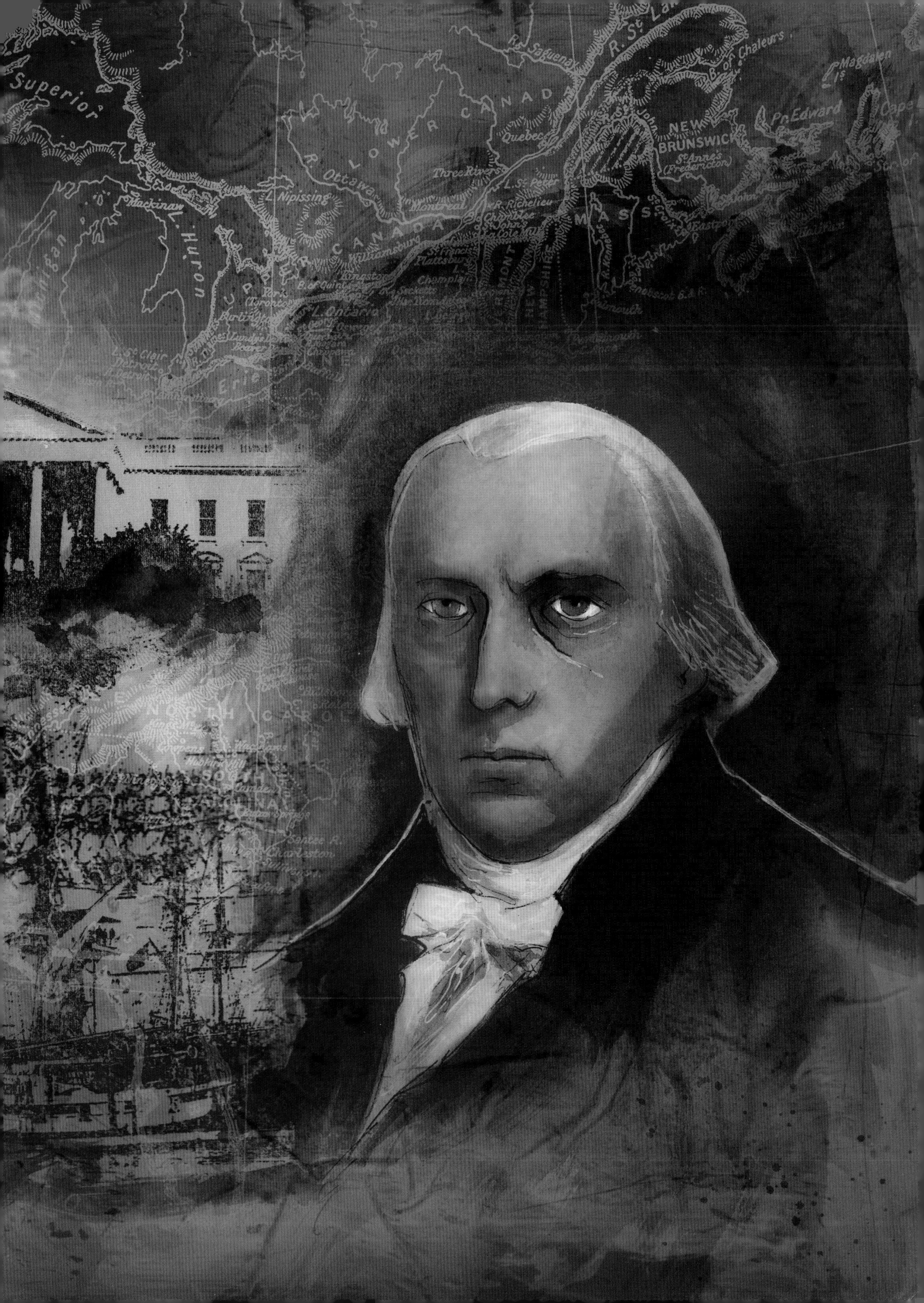
Superior
LOWER CANADA
R. Saguenay
B. of Chaleurs
Magdalen Is
Pr. Edward
NEW BRUNSWICK
Quebec
Three Rivers
R. Ottawa
L. Nipissing
Mackinaw
Montreal
R. Richelieu
L. St. Peter
Huron
CANADA
UPPER
Williamsburg
Plattsburg
Kingston
Champlain
MASS
L. Ontario
Erie
NORTH
SOUTH
Santee R.
Charleston

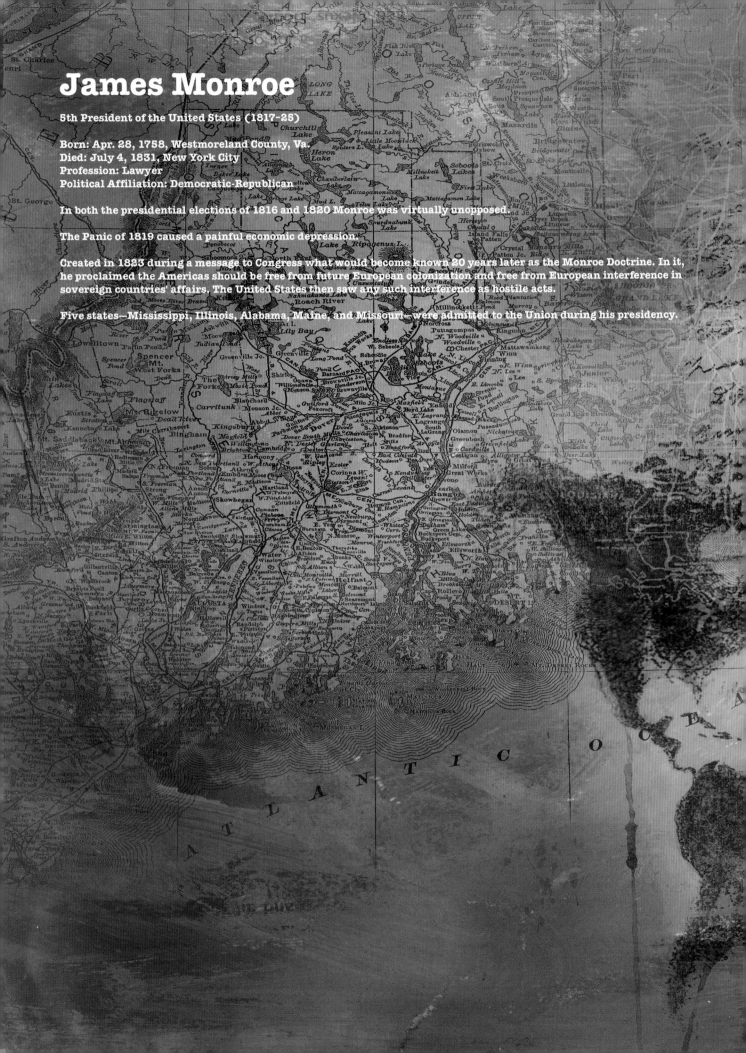

James Monroe

5th President of the United States (1817-25)

Born: Apr. 28, 1758, Westmoreland County, Va.
Died: July 4, 1831, New York City
Profession: Lawyer
Political Affiliation: Democratic-Republican

In both the presidential elections of 1816 and 1820 Monroe was virtually unopposed.

The Panic of 1819 caused a painful economic depression.

Created in 1823 during a message to Congress what would become known 20 years later as the Monroe Doctrine. In it, he proclaimed the Americas should be free from future European colonization and free from European interference in sovereign countries' affairs. The United States then saw any such interference as hostile acts.

Five states—Mississippi, Illinois, Alabama, Maine, and Missouri—were admitted to the Union during his presidency.

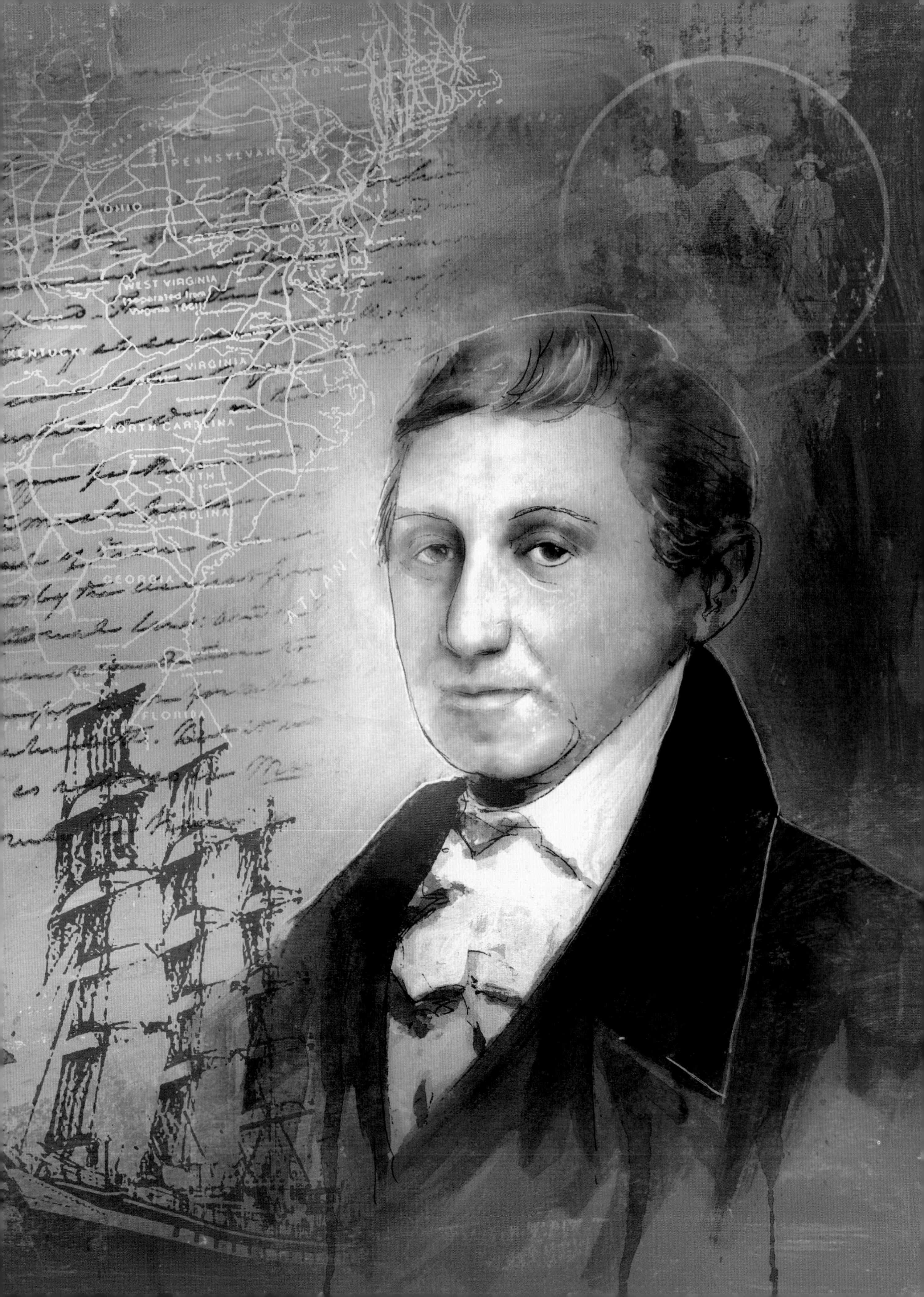
NEW YORK
PENNSYLVANIA
OHIO
WEST VIRGINIA
KENTUCKY
VIRGINIA
NORTH CAROLINA
SOUTH
CAROLINA
GEORGIA
FLORIDA
ATLANTIC

John Quincy Adams

6th President of the United States (1825-29)

Born: July 11, 1767, Braintree (now Quincy), Mass.
Died: Feb. 23, 1848, Washington, D.C.
Profession: Lawyer
Political Affiliation: Federalist; Democratic-Republican; Whig

The son of John Adams, 2nd President of the United States.

Took the oath of office on a book of laws, instead of the traditional Bible.

Despite extensive opposition, Adams had roads and canals built including the extension of the Cumberland Road into Ohio, the beginning of the Chesapeake and Ohio Canal, the construction of the Delaware and Chesapeake Canal, and the Portland to Louisville Canal.

Together with Henry Clay, he set up the National Republican Party, but it never took root in the states.

He was one of only three presidents who chose not to attend their respective successor's inauguration, after successor Andrew Jackson openly snubbed him by refusing to pay the traditional "courtesy call" to the outgoing president during the weeks before his own inauguration.

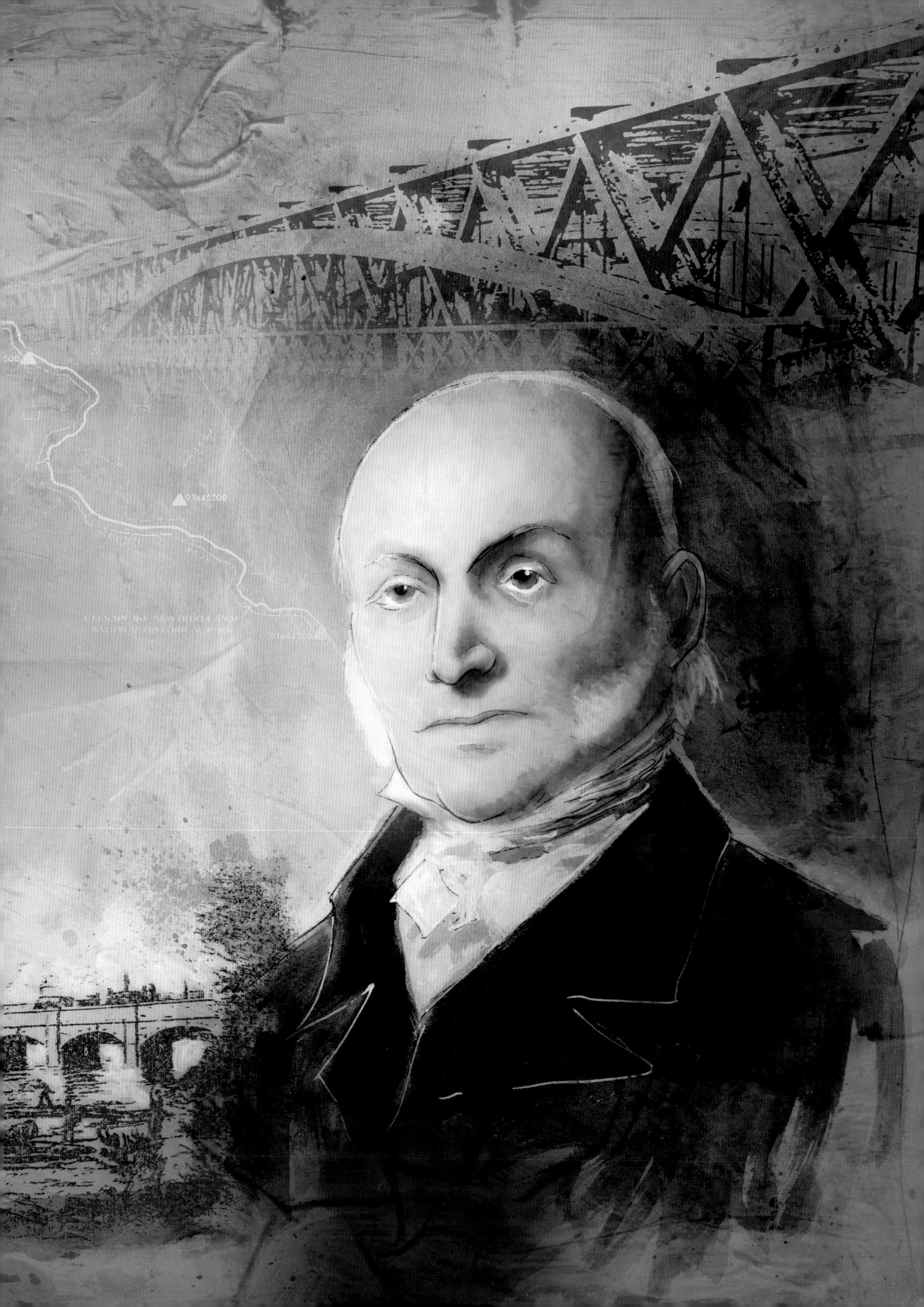
01645000

Andrew Jackson

7th President of the United States (1829-37)

Born: Mar. 15, 1767, Waxhaw area, on N.C.-S.C. border
Died: June 8, 1845, Nashville, Tenn.
Profession: Lawyer, Soldier
Political Affiliation: Democrat

During the election of 1828, Jackson's opponents referred to him as a "jackass." Jackson liked the name and used the jackass as a symbol for some time. It eventually became the symbol for the Democratic Party when cartoons popularized it.

Jackson was the first president to invite the public to attend the White House ball during his first inauguration.

Heavily reduced the federal debt until a depression from 1837 to 1844 caused it to increase to over ten times what it had previously been.

He repeatedly called for the abolition of the Electoral College by constitutional amendment.

Eventually managed to destroy the Second Bank of the United States by vetoing its 1832 re-charter by Congress and by withdrawing U.S. funds in 1833. Money lending was handed over to small local banks and the economy initially boomed, but many banks eventually collapsed precipitating the Panic of 1837.

Dealt with the "Nullification Crisis," or "secession crisis," of 1828-1832, which merged issues of sectional strife with disagreements over tariffs.

He was a leading advocate of a policy known as Indian removal in what would eventually become known as the "Trail of Tears."

The first assassination attempt on a president was against Jackson on January 30, 1835 by Richard Lawrence, an unemployed housepainter from England who blamed the president for his job loss. Lawrence aimed two pistols at Jackson, but both misfired, apparently due to the humidity. He was found insane and institutionalized.

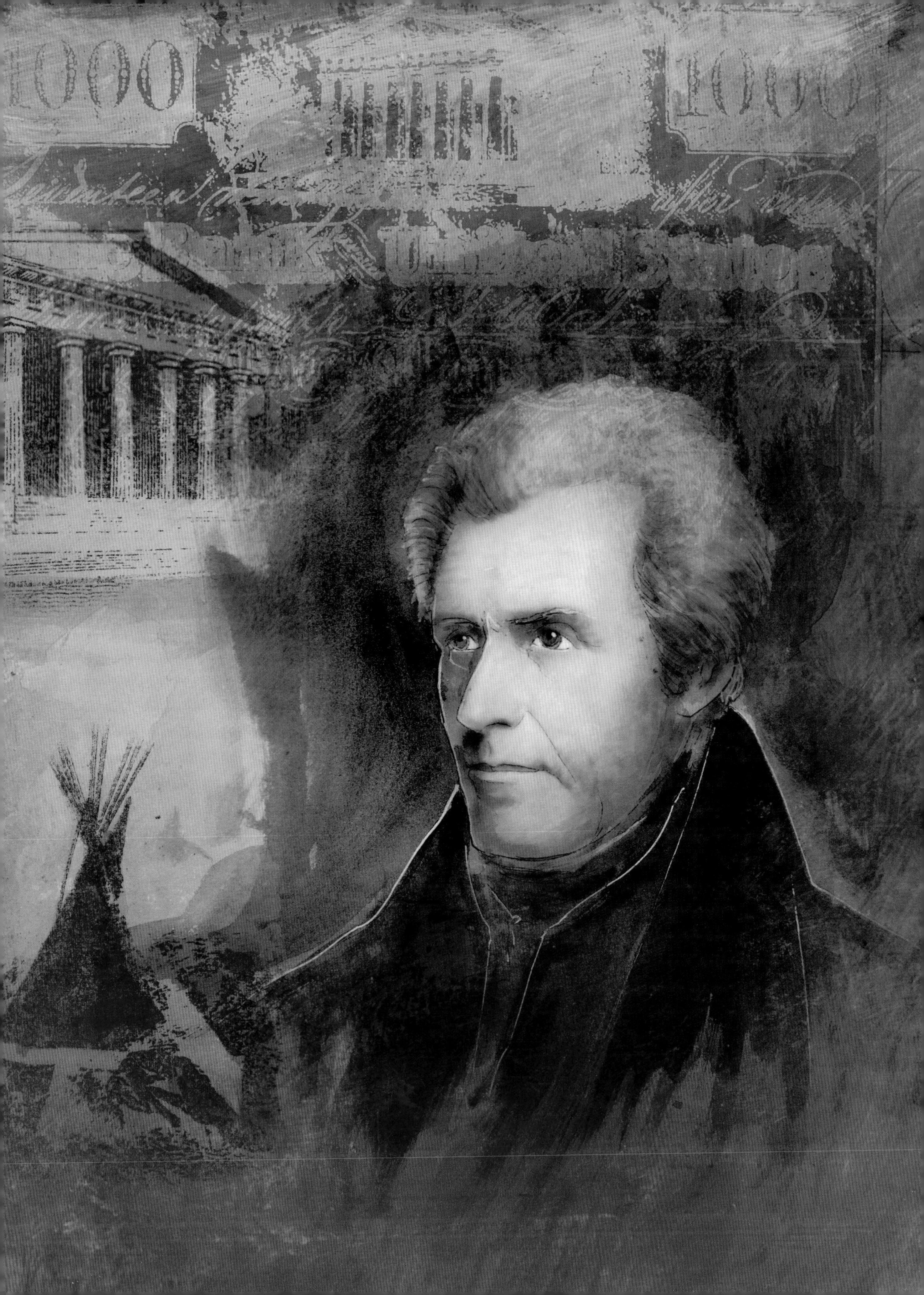

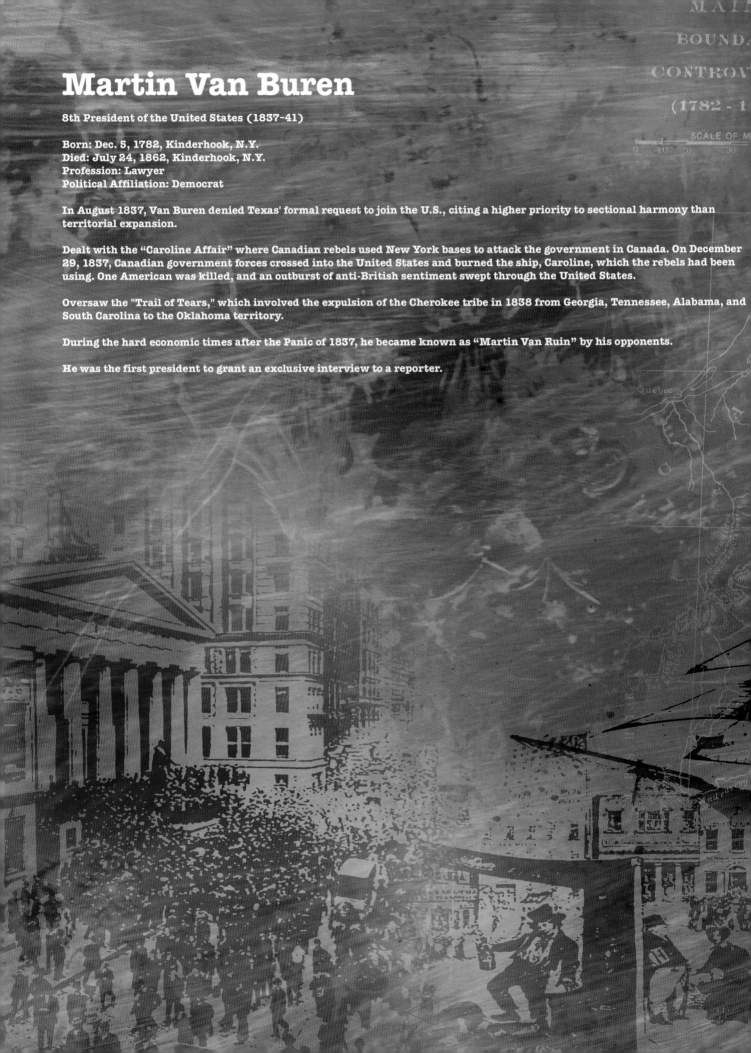

Martin Van Buren

8th President of the United States (1837-41)

Born: Dec. 5, 1782, Kinderhook, N.Y.
Died: July 24, 1862, Kinderhook, N.Y.
Profession: Lawyer
Political Affiliation: Democrat

In August 1837, Van Buren denied Texas' formal request to join the U.S., citing a higher priority to sectional harmony than territorial expansion.

Dealt with the "Caroline Affair" where Canadian rebels used New York bases to attack the government in Canada. On December 29, 1837, Canadian government forces crossed into the United States and burned the ship, Caroline, which the rebels had been using. One American was killed, and an outburst of anti-British sentiment swept through the United States.

Oversaw the "Trail of Tears," which involved the expulsion of the Cherokee tribe in 1838 from Georgia, Tennessee, Alabama, and South Carolina to the Oklahoma territory.

During the hard economic times after the Panic of 1837, he became known as "Martin Van Ruin" by his opponents.

He was the first president to grant an exclusive interview to a reporter.

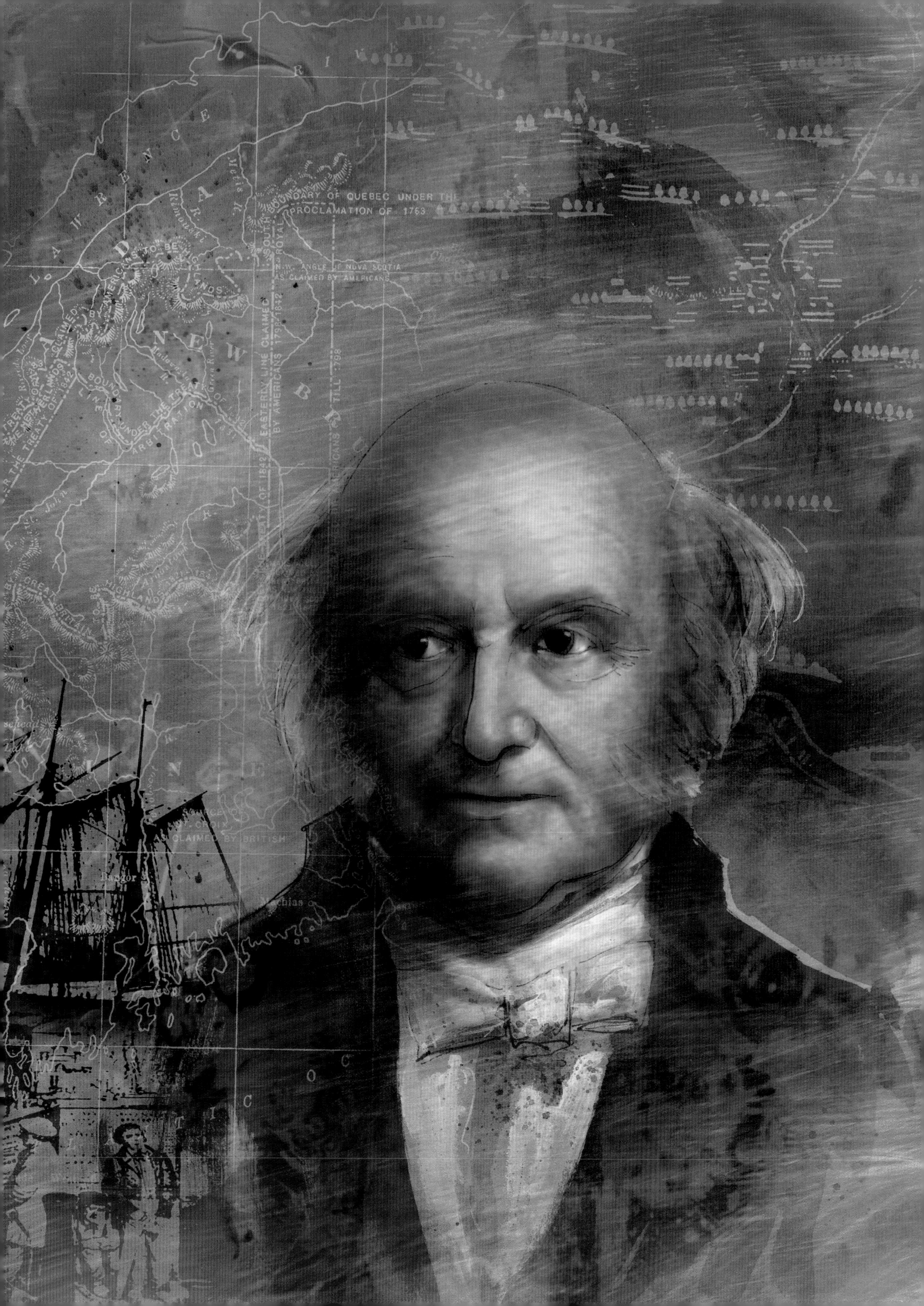

BOUNDARY OF QUEBEC UNDER THE PROCLAMATION OF 1763
N.W. ANGLE OF NOVA SCOTIA AS CLAIMED BY AMERICANS
HIGHLANDS
NEW
CLAIMED BY BRITISH
Bangor
Machias

William Henry Harrison

9th President of the United States (Mar. 4, 1841 to Apr. 4, 1841)

Born: Feb. 9, 1773, Berkeley plantation, Charles City County, Va.
Died: Apr. 4, 1841, Washington, D.C.
Profession: Soldier
Political Affiliation: Whig

Having a distinguished military career before being elected, Harrison came to Washington wanting to show he was still the steadfast hero of Tippecanoe. His inauguration was held on an extremely cold and wet day. He faced the weather without his overcoat and delivered the longest inaugural address in American history, at nearly two hours.

Slightly more than three weeks after the inauguration, Harrison showed the first signs of ill health, getting a cold. The cold worsened, rapidly turning to pneumonia and pleurisy. He died nine days later.

His only act of consequence as president was to call Congress into a special session.

Harrison served the shortest term of any American president at just over 30 days.

He was the first sitting president to have his picture taken photographically.

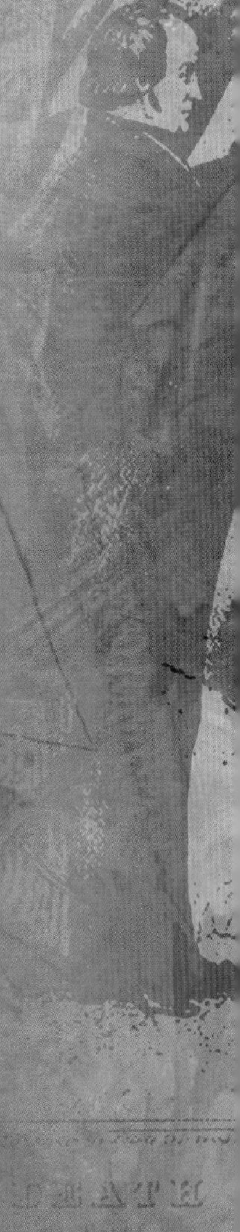

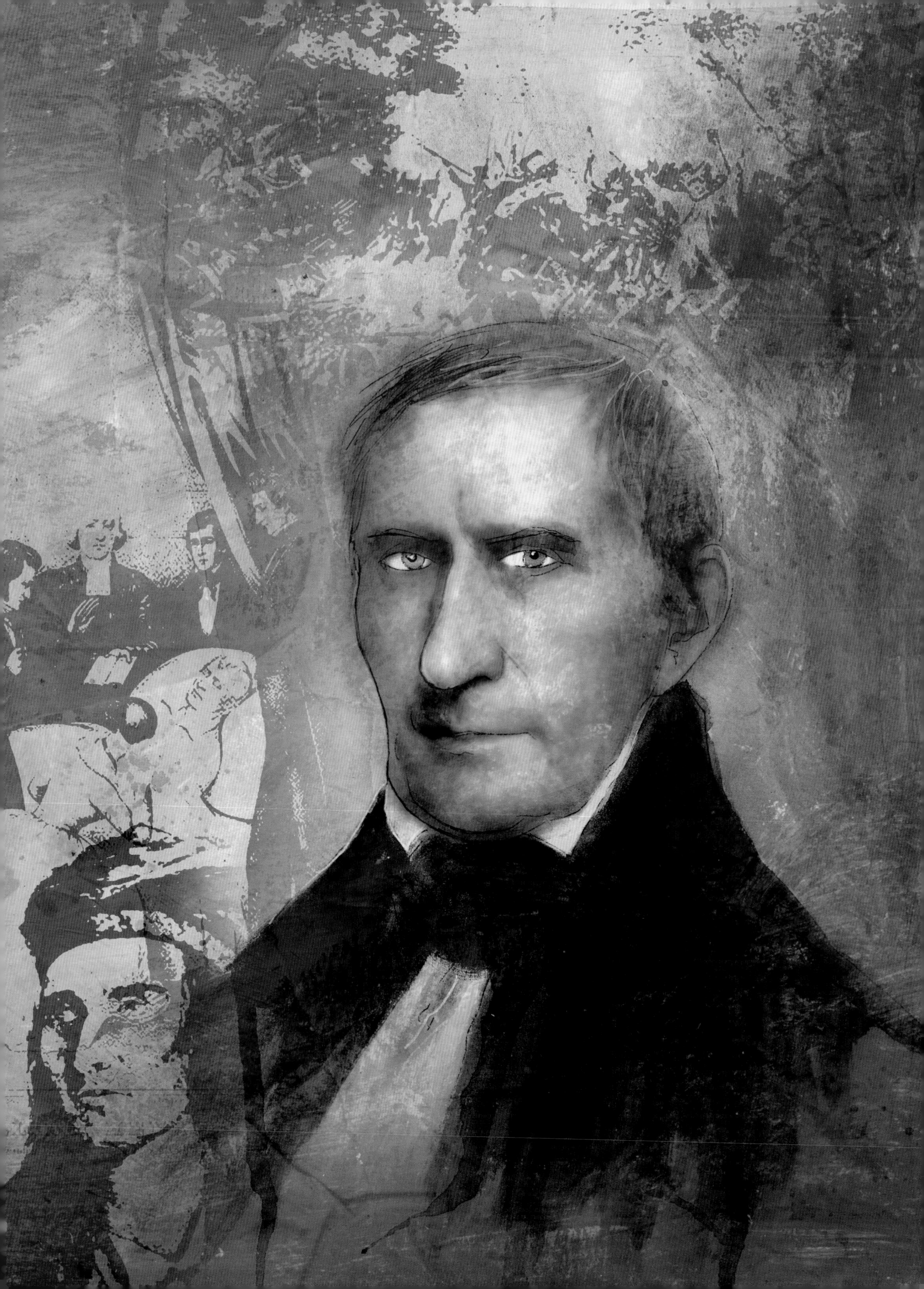

John Tyler

10th President of the United States (1841-45)

Born: Mar. 29, 1790, Charles City County, Va.
Died: Jan. 18, 1862, Richmond, Va.
Profession: Lawyer
Political Affiliation: Democrat; Whig

The first U.S. vice president to assume the office of president upon the death of his predecessor, earning him the nickname "His Accidency."

Tyler was officially expelled from the Whig Party only a few months after taking office after vetoing basically the party's entire agenda. Became the first president to have a veto overridden by Congress.

Sent a diplomatic mission to China, successfully establishing consular and commercial relations.

In 1843, after he vetoed a tariff bill, the House of Representatives considered the first impeachment resolution against a president in American history.

Signed the bill that annexed the independent Republic of Texas three days before he was due to leave office.

On his last full day in office, March 3, 1845, Florida was admitted to the Union.

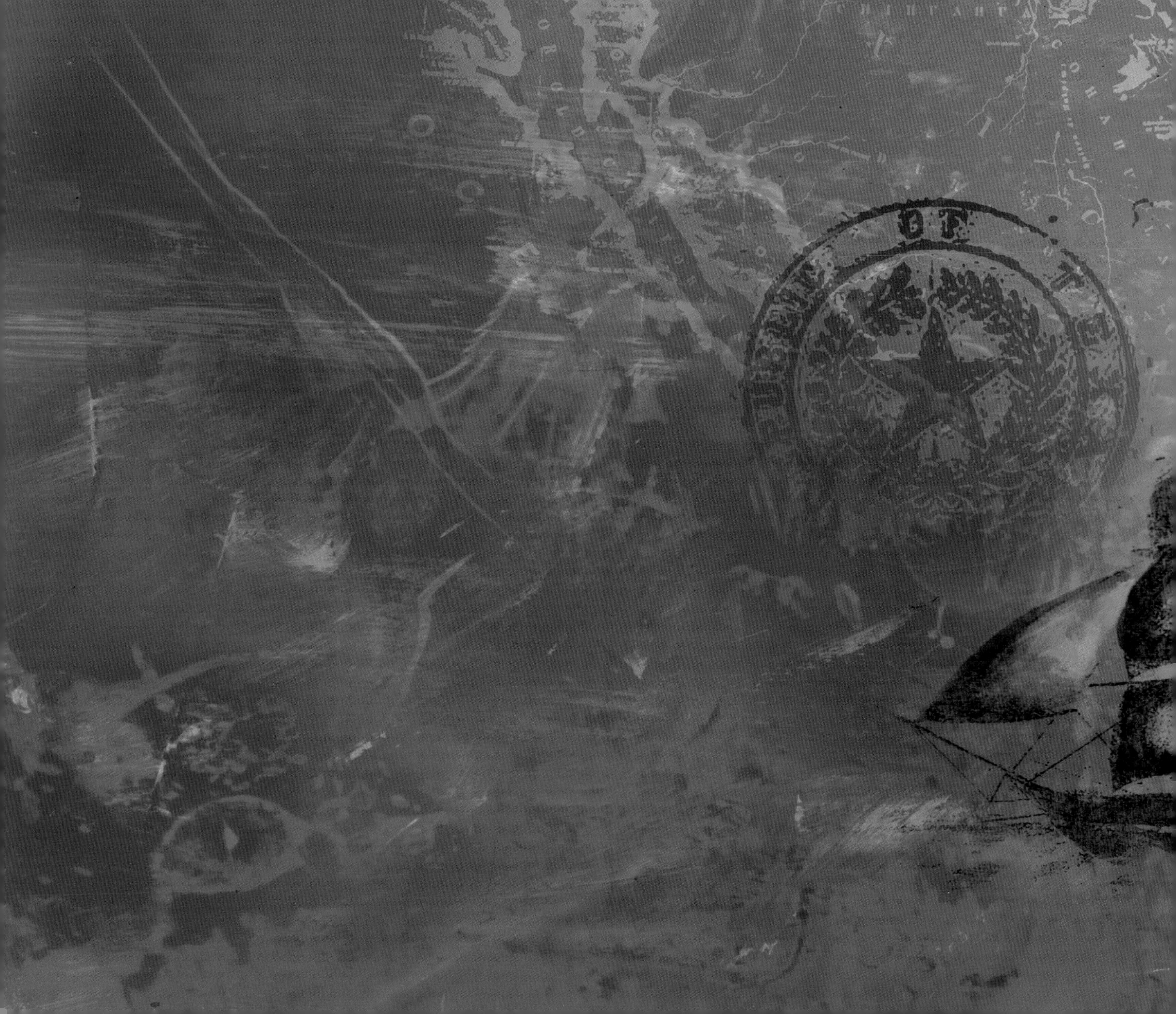

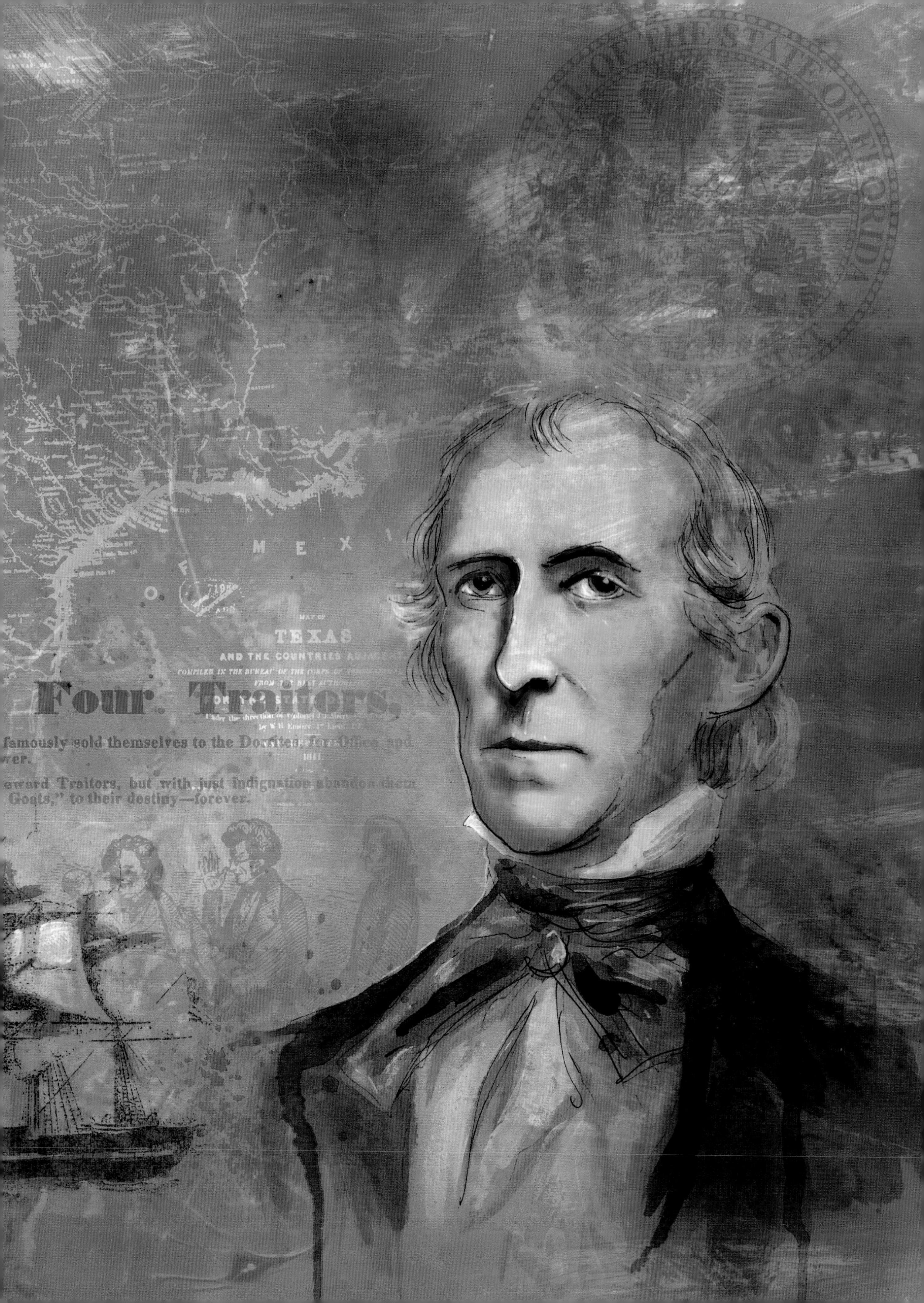
M E X I
MAP OF
TEXAS
AND THE COUNTRIES ADJACENT
Four Traitors,
famously sold themselves to the Dorrites, for Office and
wer.
eward Traitors, but with just indignation abandon them
Goats," to their destiny—forever.
1844

James K. Polk

11th President of the United States (1845-49)

Born: Nov. 2, 1795, Mecklenburg County, N.C.
Died: June 15, 1849, Nashville, Tenn.
Profession: Lawyer
Political Affiliation: Democrat

When he came to office in 1845, Polk, at 49, became the youngest man at the time to assume the presidency.

He promised to serve only one term as president, and did.

Polk was a slaveholder for his entire life. During his presidency, many abolitionists harshly criticized him as an instrument of the "Slave Power."

Texas officially became a state on December 29, 1845, angering Mexico which still claimed it and warned that annexation would lead to war.

Tried to buy California and New Mexico from Mexico for 20 to 30 million dollars. This was rebuffed and seen as an insult by the United States, which further angered Mexico who had anticipated an offer of compensation for the loss of Texas.

After Mexican troops crossed the Rio Grande area and killed eleven American soldiers, Polk declared war. Following various defeats and the capture of Mexico City, the United States and Mexico finally agreed to peace terms set out by Polk in 1848 in the Treaty of Guadalupe Hidalgo, halving the size of Mexico and increasing the size of the U.S. by a third.

Tried unsuccessfully to buy Cuba from Spain for the then unheard of sum of 100 million dollars.

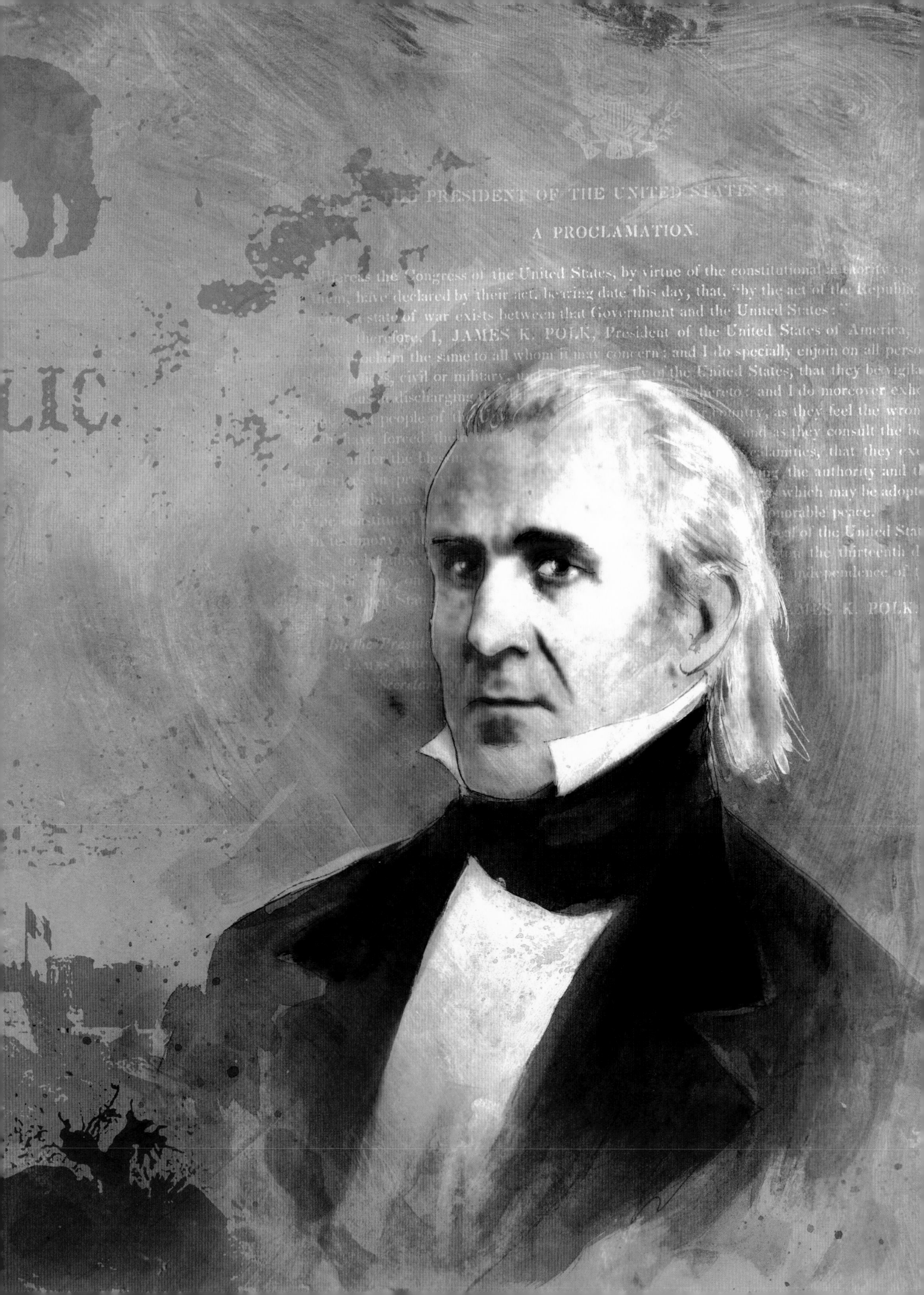

PRESIDENT OF THE UNITED STATES
A PROCLAMATION.
the Congress of the United States, by virtue of the constitutional
have declared by their act, bearing date this day, that, "by the act of the Republic
state of war exists between that Government and the United States:"
therefore, I, JAMES K. POLK, President of the United States of America,
the same to all whom it may concern; and I do specially enjoin on all perso
civil or military, of the United States, that they be vigila
and I do moreover exh
country, as they feel the wron
and as they consult the b
calamities, that they ex
the authority and t
which may be adopt
honorable peace.
of the United Sta
the thirteenth d
independence of
JAMES K. POLK.
LIC

Zachary Taylor

12th President of the United States (1849-50)

Born: Nov. 24, 1784, near Barboursville, Va.
Died: July 9, 1850, Washington, D.C.
Profession: Soldier
Political Affiliation: Whig

A hero of the Mexican-American War.

A slave owner, he was a moderate on the issue of slavery and proposed the complex Compromise of 1850 between northern and southern states. Taylor died on July 9, 1850, as it was being debated. Though somewhat unclear, the cause was listed as gastroenteritis.

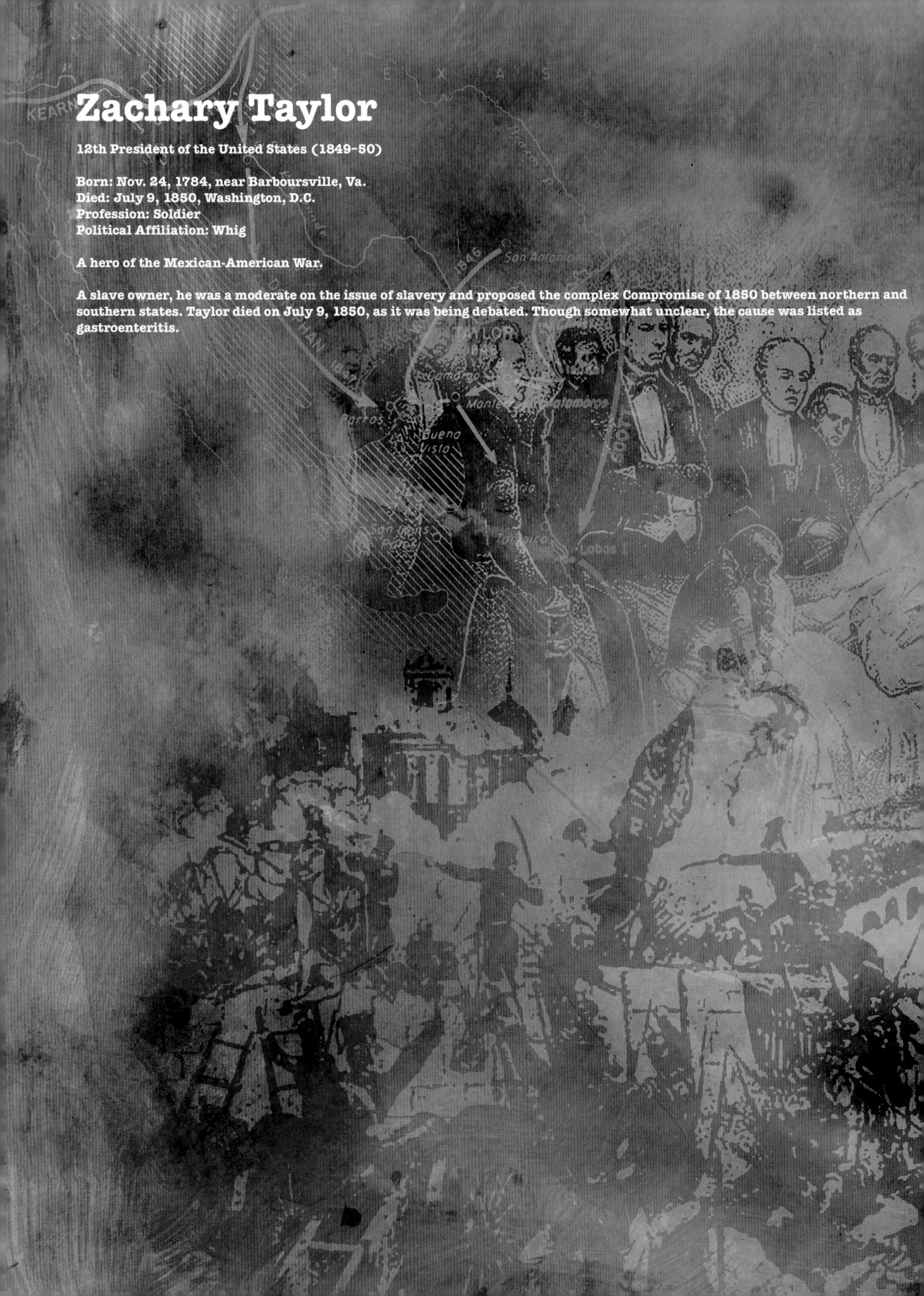

T E X A S
1846
San Antonio
Camargo
Parras
Buena Vista
Victoria
Tampico

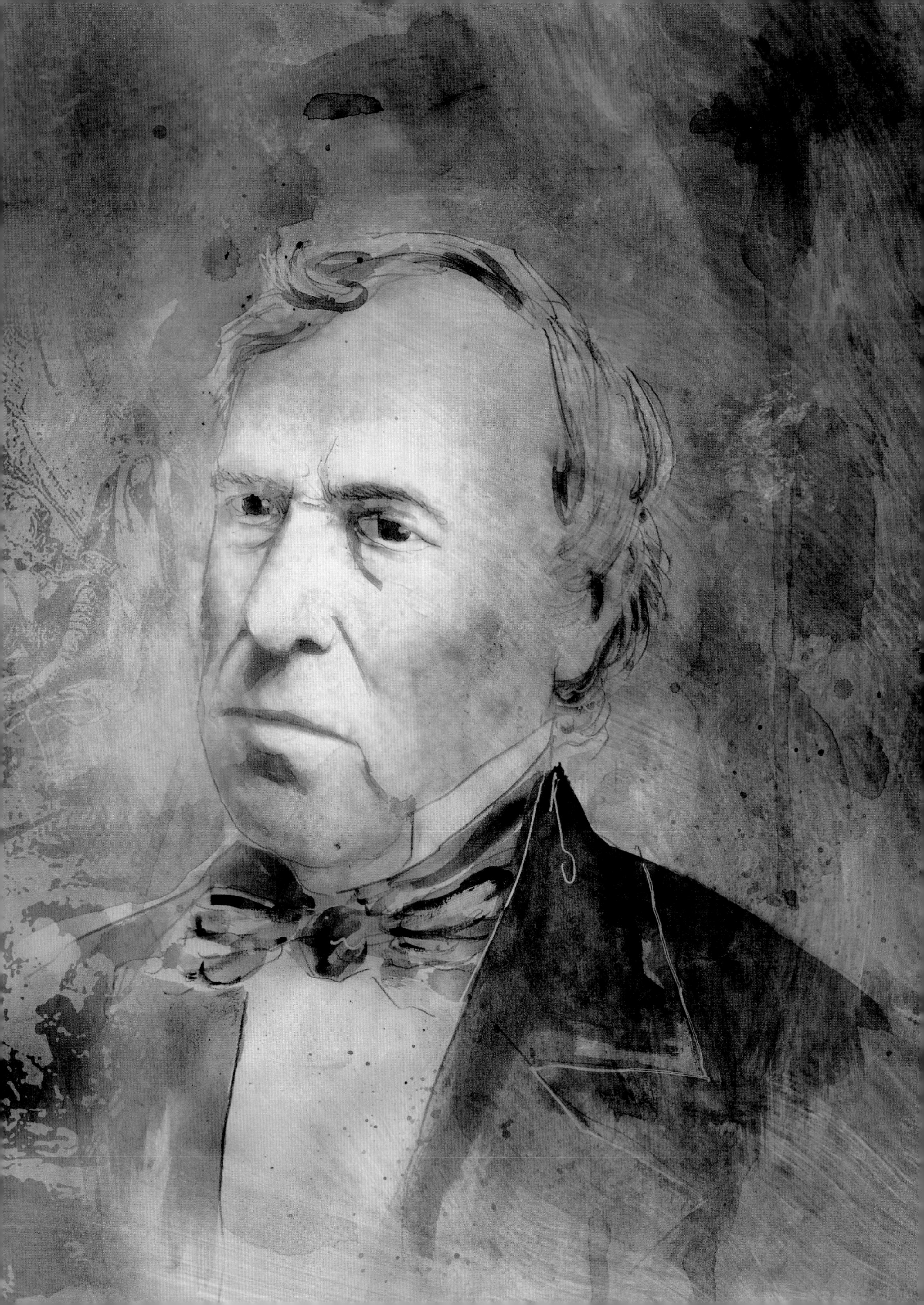

Millard Fillmore

13th President of the United States (1850-53)

Born: Jan. 7, 1800, Summerhill, N.Y.
Died: Mar. 8, 1874, Buffalo, N.Y.
Profession: Lawyer
Political Affiliation: Whig

The last member of the Whig Party to ever hold the office.

Signed legislation to admit California to the Union as a free (non-slave) state, made New Mexico a territory, placed federal officers at the disposal of slaveholders seeking escapees with the Fugitive Slave Act, and abolished slavery in the District of Columbia.

Fillmore appointed Brigham Young as the first governor of the Utah Territory in 1850.

Sent Commodore Matthew C. Perry to open Japan to Western trade, though Perry did not reach Japan during Fillmore's presidency.

The myth that Millard Fillmore installed the White House's first bathtub was started in a newspaper joke column in 1917.

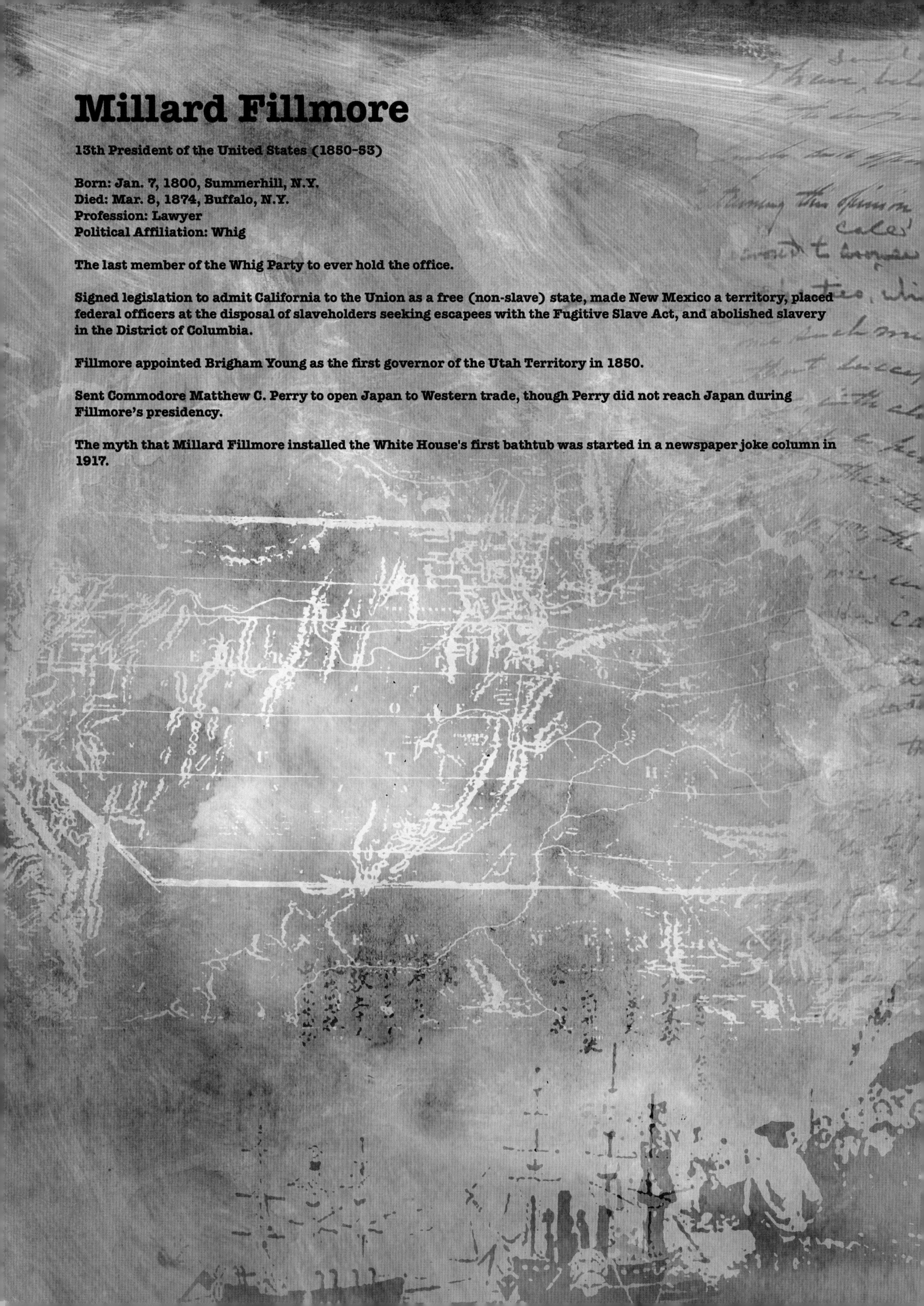

from the first, ...

... the country the present ...

... so great a disaster, but ... has been permitted to ... to resist it, until it ... no longer be dis... ... danger. I have ... ... the gravest question ... your consideration, ... be preserved? ... ... mighty question, it ... ... the nature and the ... ... knowledge it ... ... by what means it ca ... ... for a ... ... danger ...

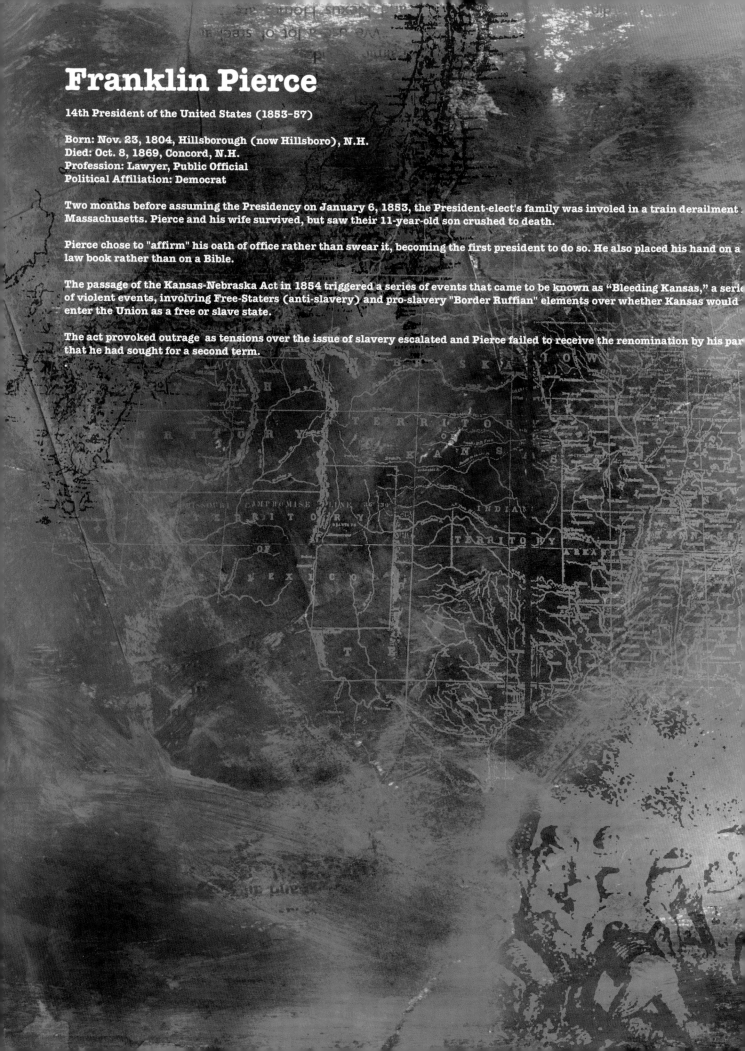

Franklin Pierce

14th President of the United States (1853-57)

Born: Nov. 23, 1804, Hillsborough (now Hillsboro), N.H.
Died: Oct. 8, 1869, Concord, N.H.
Profession: Lawyer, Public Official
Political Affiliation: Democrat

Two months before assuming the Presidency on January 6, 1853, the President-elect's family was involed in a train derailment
Massachusetts. Pierce and his wife survived, but saw their 11-year-old son crushed to death.

Pierce chose to "affirm" his oath of office rather than swear it, becoming the first president to do so. He also placed his hand on a
law book rather than on a Bible.

The passage of the Kansas-Nebraska Act in 1854 triggered a series of events that came to be known as "Bleeding Kansas," a series
of violent events, involving Free-Staters (anti-slavery) and pro-slavery "Border Ruffian" elements over whether Kansas would
enter the Union as a free or slave state.

The act provoked outrage as tensions over the issue of slavery escalated and Pierce failed to receive the renomination by his party
that he had sought for a second term.

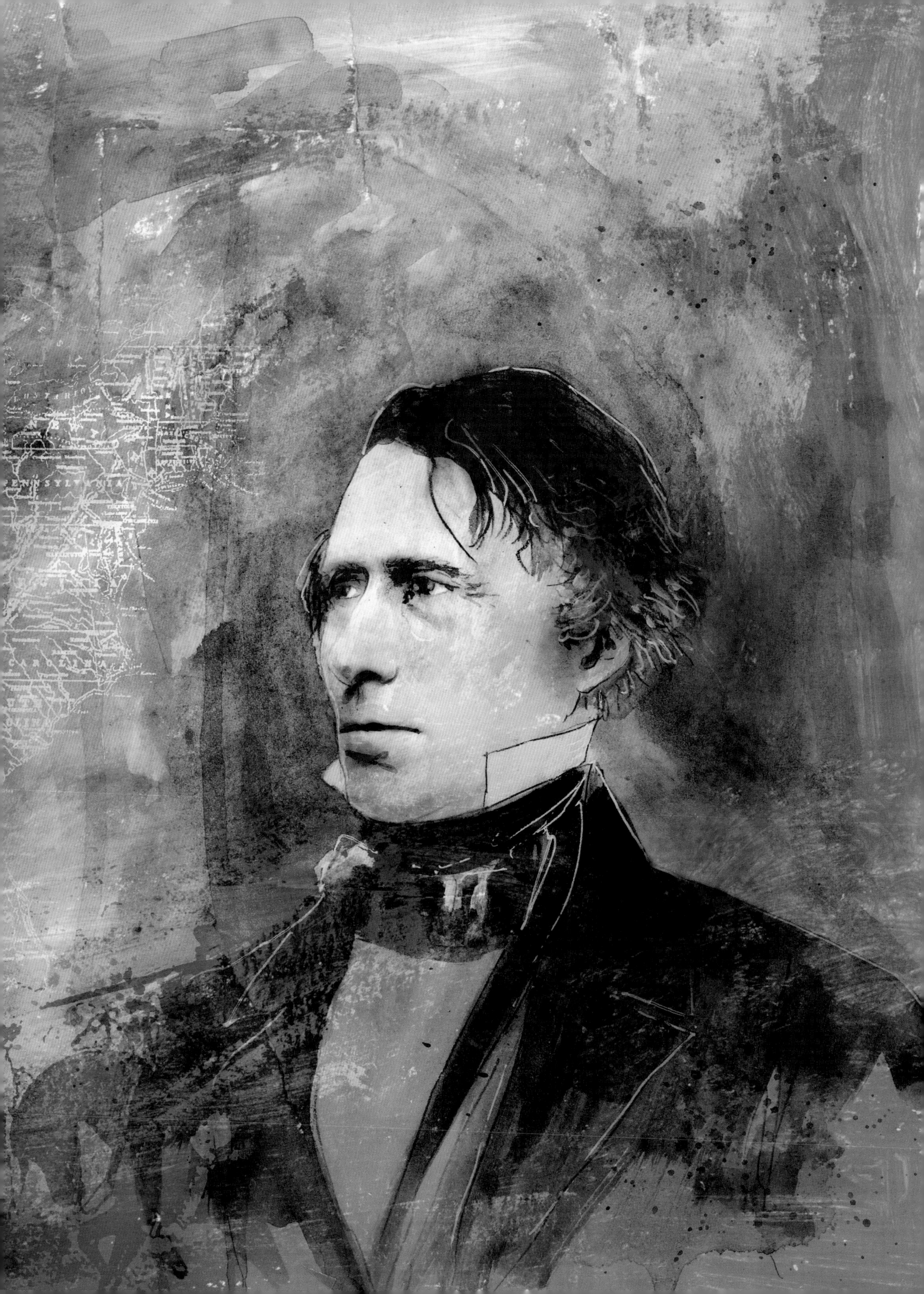
PENNSYLVANIA
CAROLINA

James Buchanan

15th President of the United States (1857-61)

Born: Apr. 23, 1791, Cove Gap (near Mercersburg), Pa.
Died: June 1, 1868, near Lancaster, Pa.
Profession: Lawyer
Political Affiliation: Democrat

Buchanan was known as a "doughface," a northern man with southern principles.

Dealt with the Panic of 1857 after the boom caused by the Mexican-American war and gold discoveries in California waned.

The Republican Party won a plurality in the House in 1856, after which every significant bill they passed fell before Southern votes in the Senate or a presidential veto. The federal government reached a stalemate.

In 1860, with tensions between the northern and southern states riding high, Buchanan's Democratic party split. He did nothing as South Carolina seceded on December 20, followed by six other cotton states, and by February they formed the Confederate States of America.

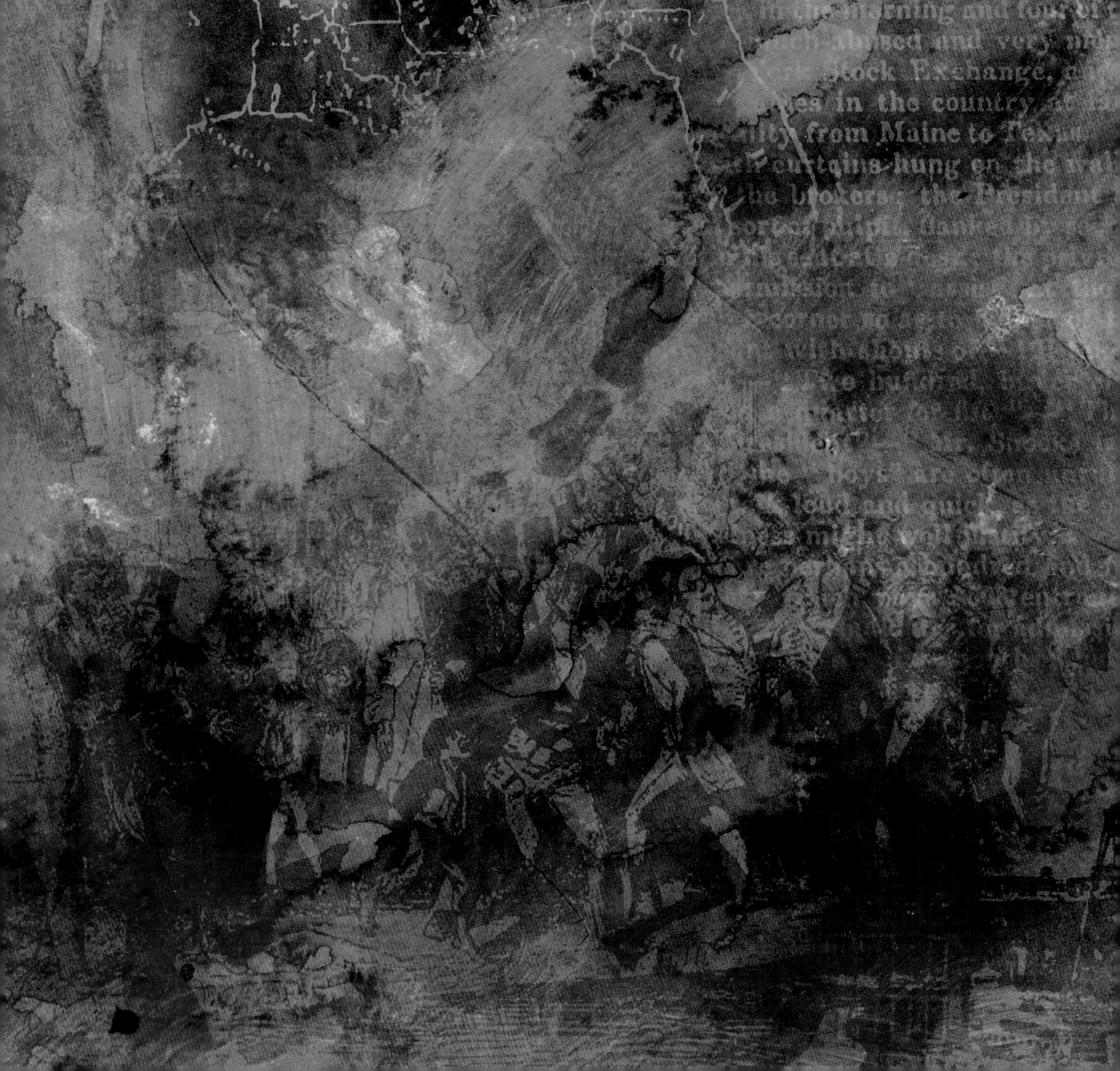

...brokers have gr...

...an aspir...

...a member...

...brokers are g...

...In cases where...

...they are usually ready en...

...quits with their debtor, and read...

Board. These men make money, e...

generous and liberal.

The normal business of the Board...

sales and purchases of stocks required by...

the public. When Brown, having saved...

wants to buy Virginia State to that amount...

directs his broker to effect the purchase...

Board; so when Smith, happening to need...

for his business, betakes himself a...

Erie into money, he intrusts his...

operation. This is the legitimate...

Stock Board.

In these lines it is a very...

Ninety-nine hundredths of...

Board have nothing whatev...

resting of savings in the com...

...into cash. The famous...

...tutes of the New York Stoc...

...bling devices. For instance...

Smith believes that Erie Rail...

...ing uncommonly cheap. He...

...mediately and makes his...

...of weeks Erie...

Abraham Lincoln

16th President of the United States (1861-65)

Born: Feb. 12, 1809, Hardin (now Larue) County, Ky.
Died: Apr. 15, 1865, Washington, D.C.
Profession: Lawyer
Political Affiliation: Whig; Republican

He was the first president to be born outside the original 13 colonies.

Lincoln became the first president to have a beard while in office.

Ending slavery was always a primary goal of the Lincoln administration. However, the American public was slow to embrace the idea. He also made it subservient to the cause of preserving the union.

He decided to not take any action against the South unless the Union itself was attacked first, which happened in April 1861.

The Emancipation Proclamation, announced on September 22 and put into effect on January 1, 1863, freed slaves in territories not under Union control.

Deciding to institute a draft after horrendous casualties at the Battle of Gettysburg, Lincoln faced sentiments turning against him and the war effort, which led to his Gettysburg Address on November 19, 1863 during the dedication of the site as a war cemetery. In it, Lincoln redefined the American nation, arguing that it was born not in 1789 but in 1776, "conceived in Liberty, and dedicated to the proposition that all men are created equal."

After Union victories at Gettysburg, Vicksburg, and Chattanooga in 1863, under the command of Ulysses S. Grant, the Union began to wear down General Lee's Confederate Army.

On Good Friday, April 14, 1865, President Lincoln was shot while attending a performance of "Our American Cousin" at Ford's Theatre. He was the first president to be assassinated.

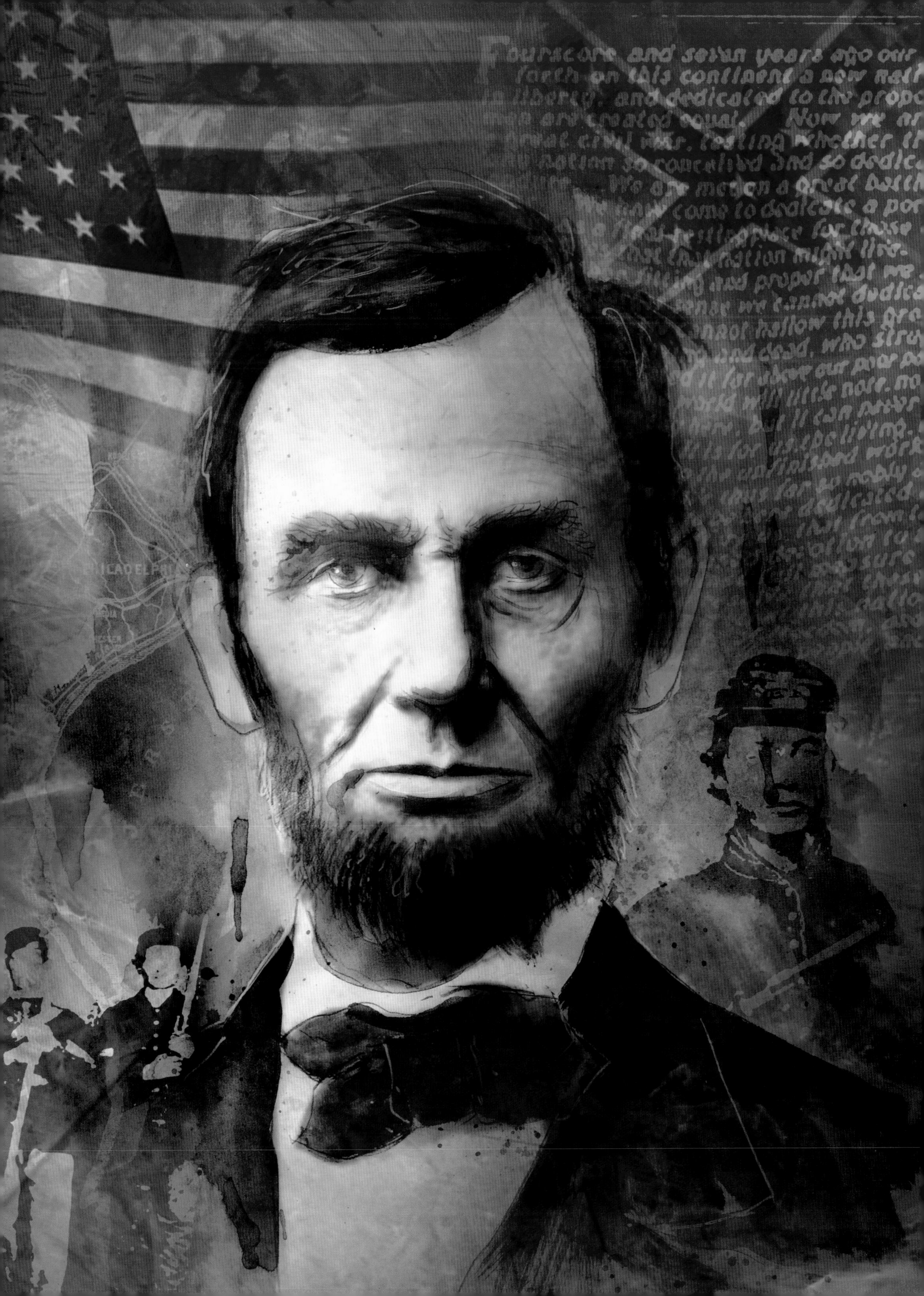

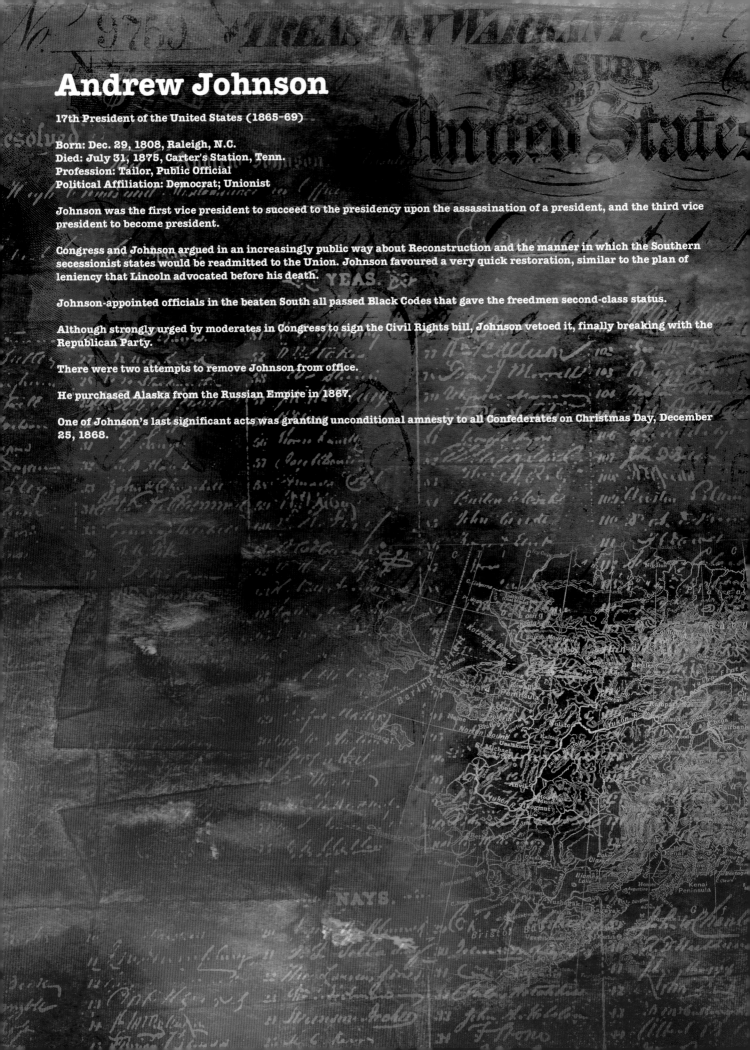

Andrew Johnson

17th President of the United States (1865-69)

Born: Dec. 29, 1808, Raleigh, N.C.
Died: July 31, 1875, Carter's Station, Tenn.
Profession: Tailor, Public Official
Political Affiliation: Democrat; Unionist

Johnson was the first vice president to succeed to the presidency upon the assassination of a president, and the third vice president to become president.

Congress and Johnson argued in an increasingly public way about Reconstruction and the manner in which the Southern secessionist states would be readmitted to the Union. Johnson favoured a very quick restoration, similar to the plan of leniency that Lincoln advocated before his death.

Johnson-appointed officials in the beaten South all passed Black Codes that gave the freedmen second-class status.

Although strongly urged by moderates in Congress to sign the Civil Rights bill, Johnson vetoed it, finally breaking with the Republican Party.

There were two attempts to remove Johnson from office.

He purchased Alaska from the Russian Empire in 1867.

One of Johnson's last significant acts was granting unconditional amnesty to all Confederates on Christmas Day, December 25, 1868.

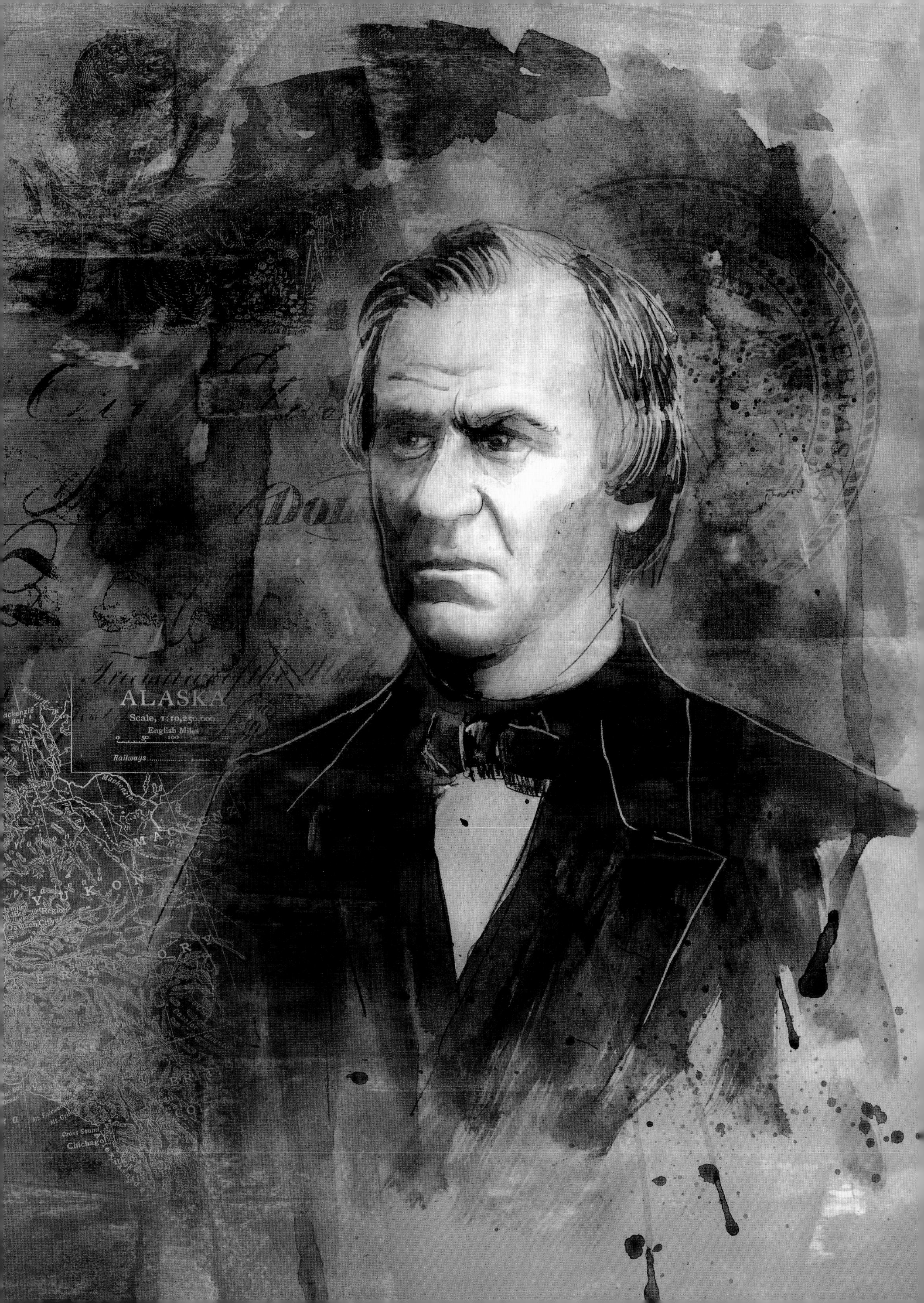
ALASKA
Scale, 1:10,250,000
English Miles
Railways
YUKON
Dawson City
NEBRASKA

Ulysses S. Grant

18th President of the United States (1869–77)

Born: Apr. 27, 1822, Point Pleasant, Ohio
Died: July 23, 1885, Mount McGregor, N.Y.
Profession: Soldier
Political Affiliation: Republican

He supported amnesty for Confederate leaders and protection for the civil rights of African-Americans.

Grant signed bills promoting voting rights and prosecuting Klan leaders. The15th Amendment to the U.S. Constitution, establishing voting rights regardless of race, was ratified in 1870.

The Panic of 1873 saw the start of a long economic depression.

Grant proposed to annex the independent, largely black nation of Santo Domingo, believing that the exodus of black labor to a safe haven would force Southern whites to realize the necessity of such a significant workforce and accept their civil rights.

Had to deal with several scandals, including the "Whiskey Ring" of 1875, in which over three million dollars in taxes were stolen from the federal government with the aid of high government officials. Although Grant himself never profited from any of the scandals, he was seen to have not taken strong action against them.

Once, while in office, he was arrested for speeding his horse and buggy, fined $20, and had to walk back to the White House.

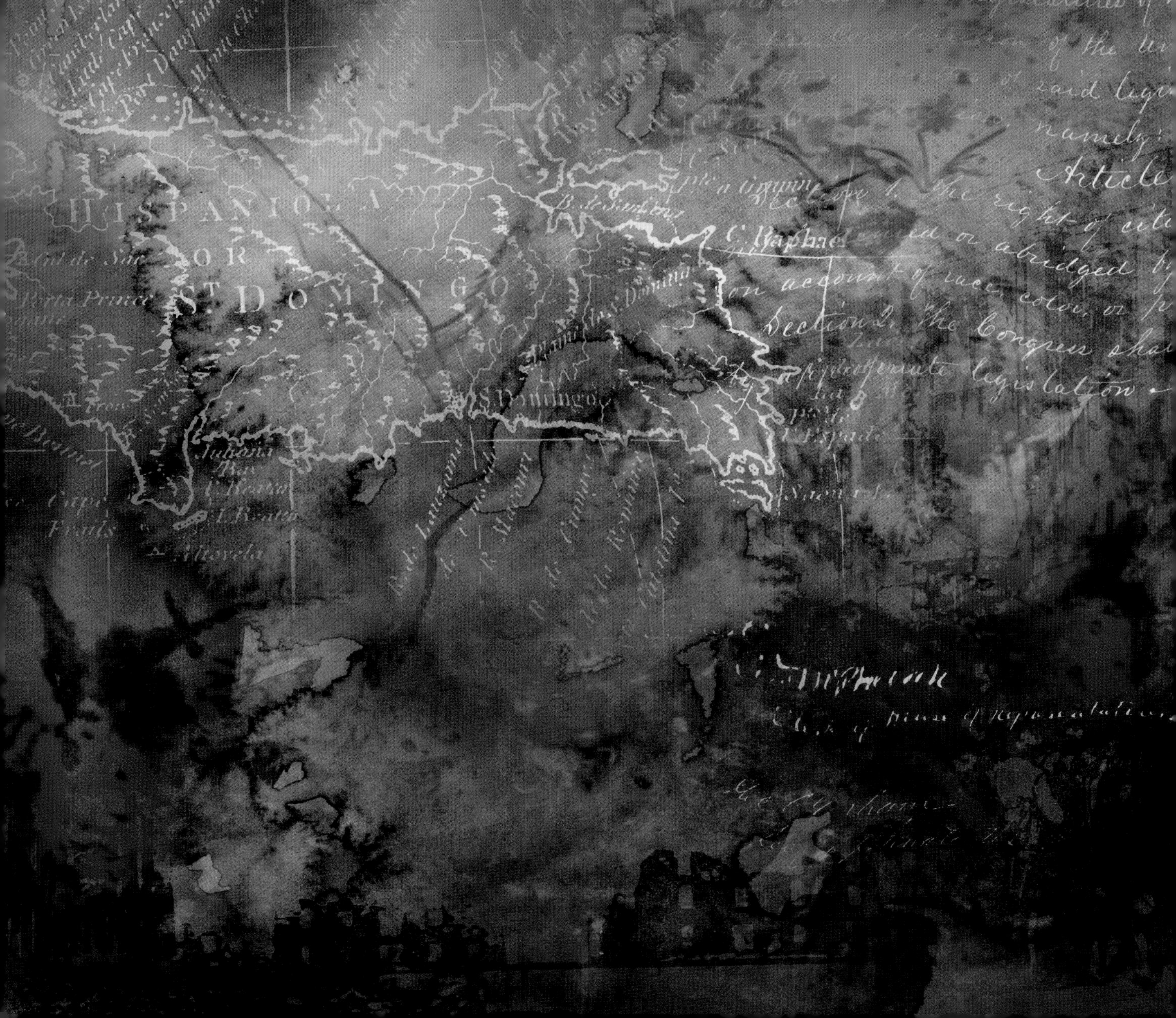

HISPANIOLA
OR
ST. DOMINGO
S. Domingo
Article

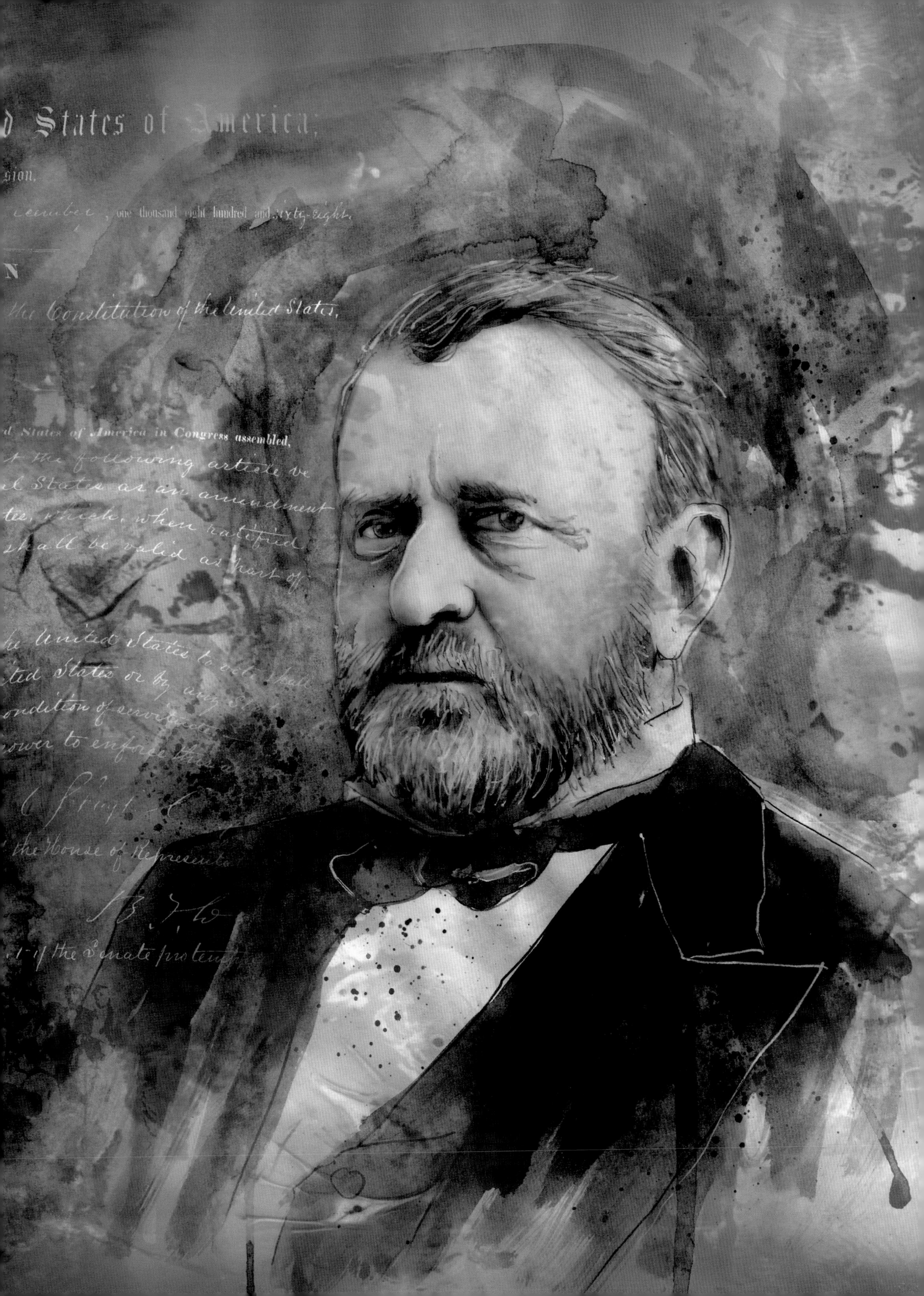
States of
one thousand eight hundred and sixty-eight.
States of America in Congress assembled,

Rutherford B. Hayes

19th President of the United States (1877-81)

Born: Oct. 4, 1822, Delaware, Ohio
Died: Jan. 17, 1893, Fremont, Ohio
Profession: Lawyer
Political Affiliation: Republican

His inauguration ceremony was held in secret, on March 4, 1877, because the previous year's election had been so bitterly divisive that outgoing President Grant feared an insurrection. Hayes was sworn in publicly on March 5.

Hayes vetoed bills repealing civil rights enforcement four times before finally signing one that satisfied his requirement for African-American rights.

During the Great Railroad Strike of 1877, when the labor disputes spread and exploded into riots in several cities, Hayes called in federal troops, who, for the first time in U.S. history, fired on the striking workers, killing more than 70.

Hayes was asked by Argentina to act as arbitrator following the War of the Triple Alliance between Argentina, Brazil, and Uruguay against Paraguay.

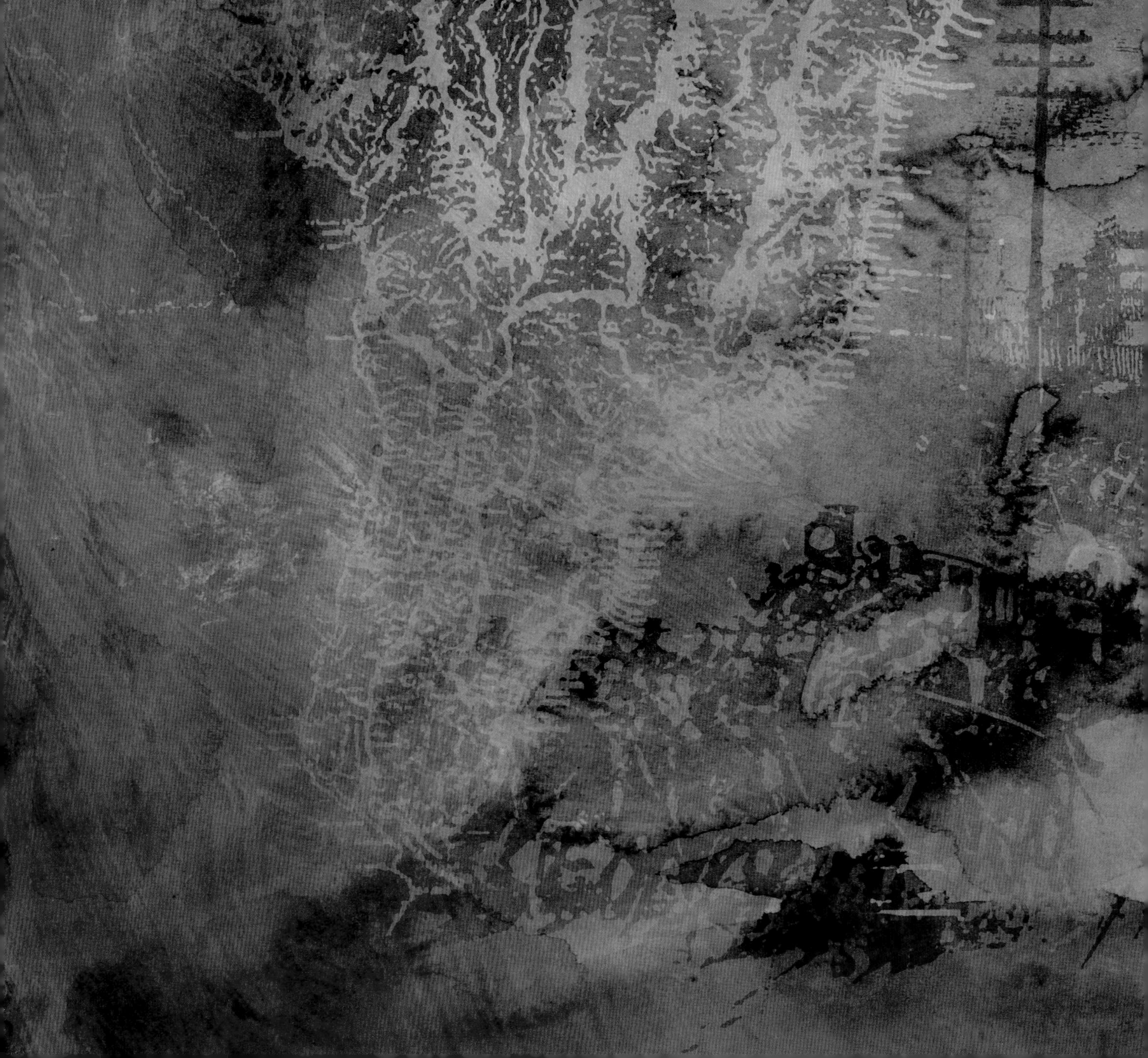

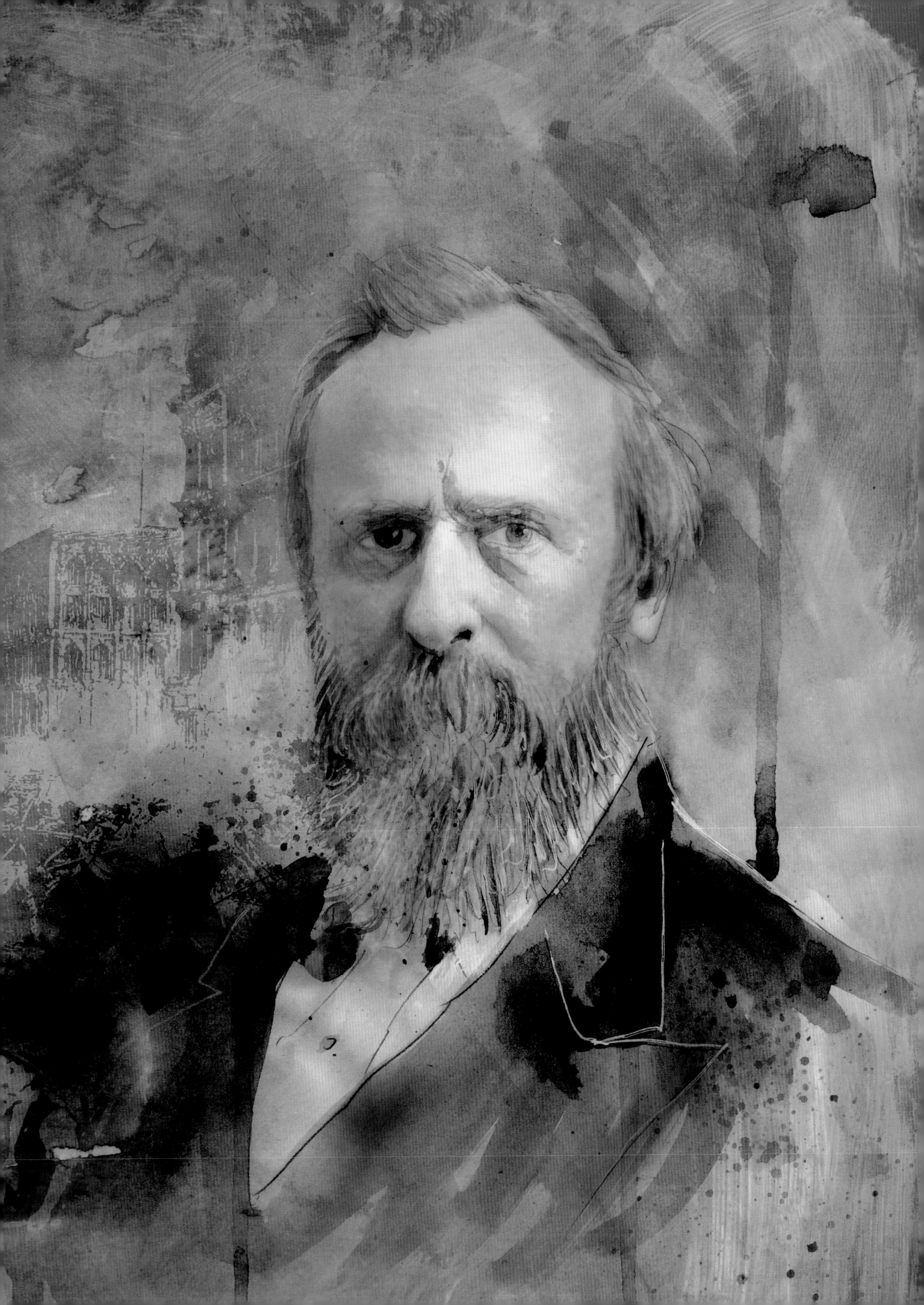

James A. Garfield

20th President of the United States (1881)

Born: Nov. 19, 1831, Orange Township, Cuyahoga County, Ohio
Died: Sept. 19, 1881, Elberon, N.J.
Profession: Teacher, Public Official
Political Affiliation: Republican

Garfield's only official social function made outside the White House was a visit to the Columbia Institution for the Deaf.

He was shot by Charles J. Guiteau, who was disgruntled by failed efforts to secure a federal post, on July 2, 1881, at 9:30 a.m. less than four months after taking office. Guiteau was sentenced to death, and was executed by hanging on June 30, 1882, his insanity defence having failed.

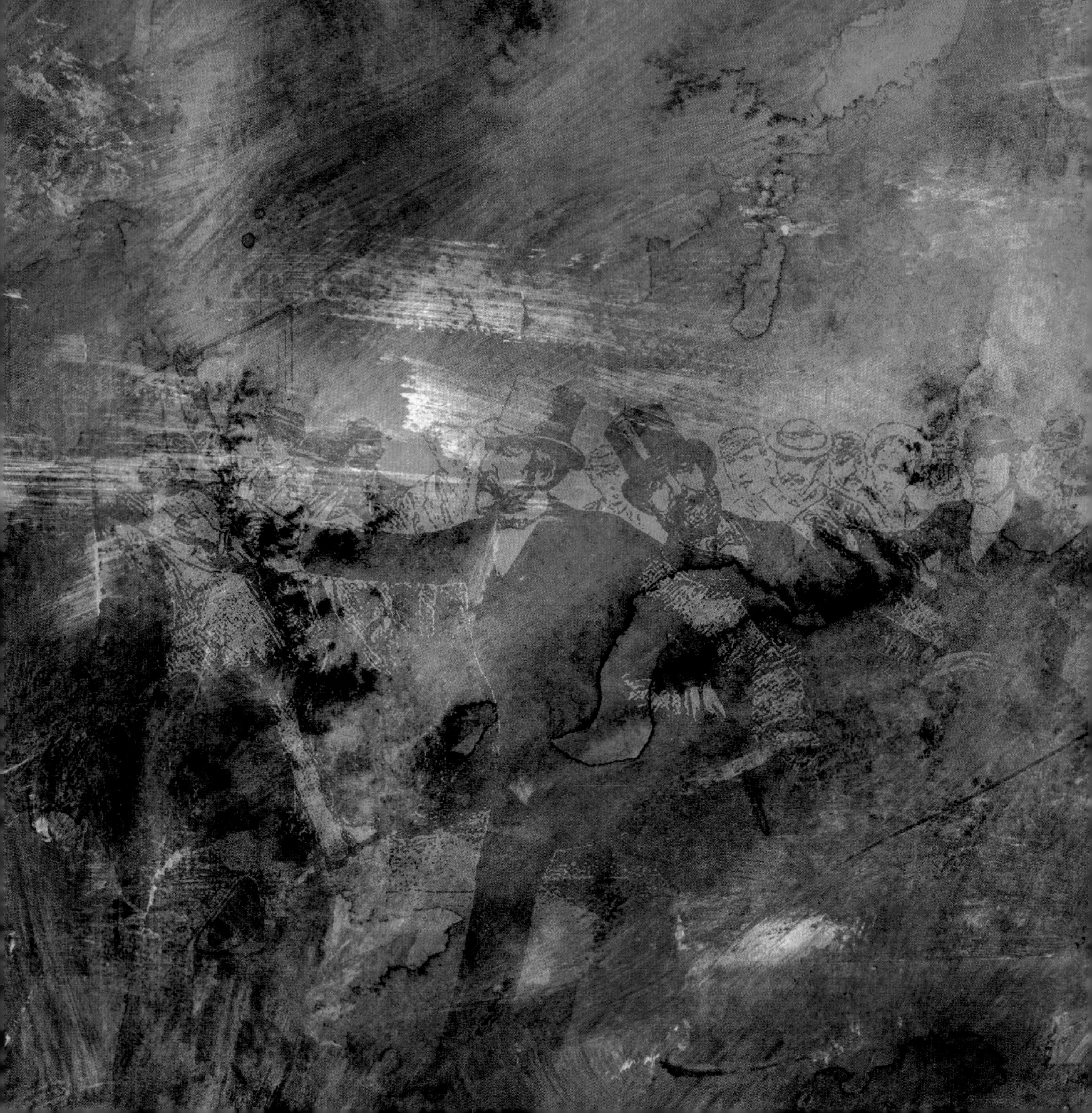

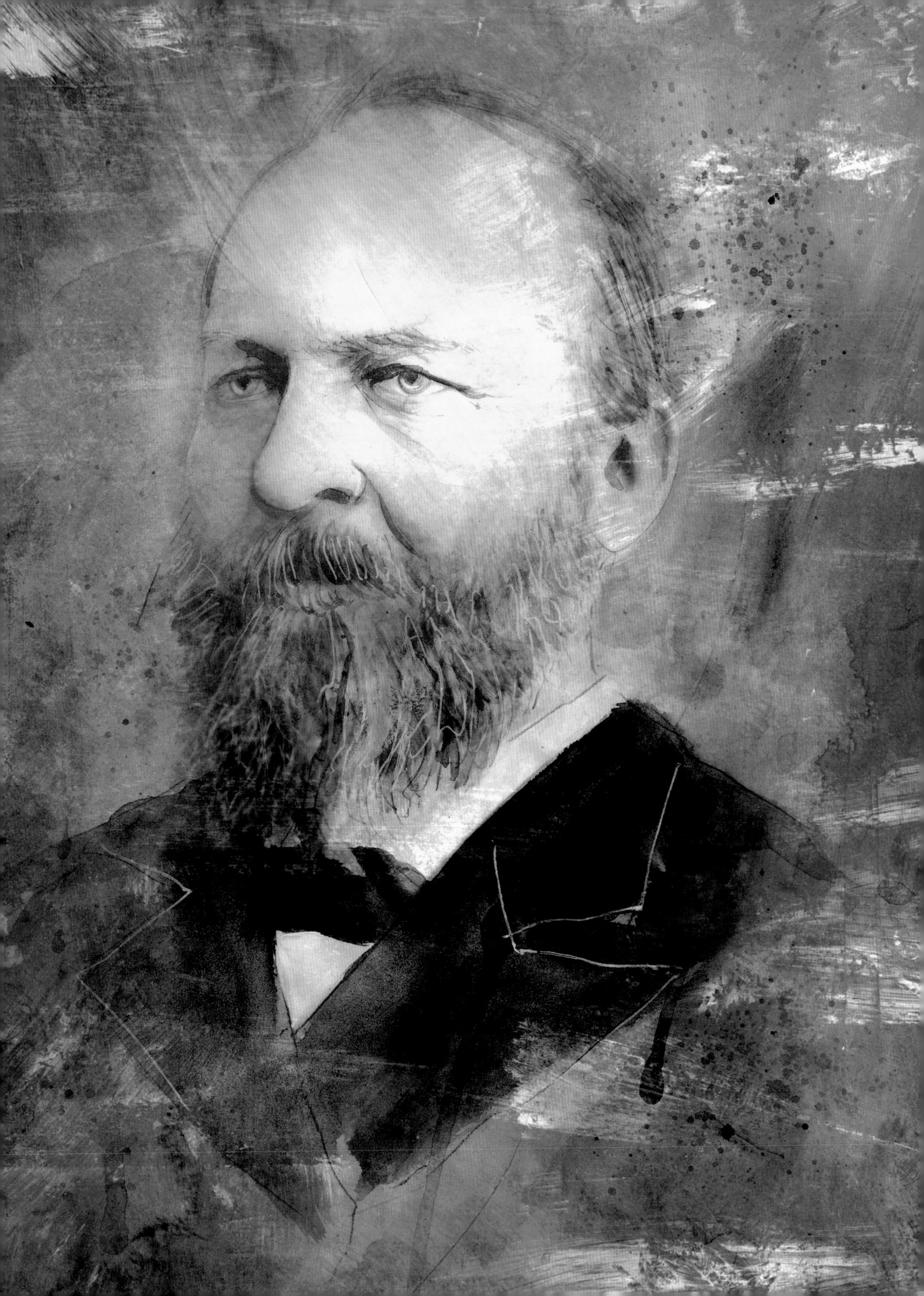

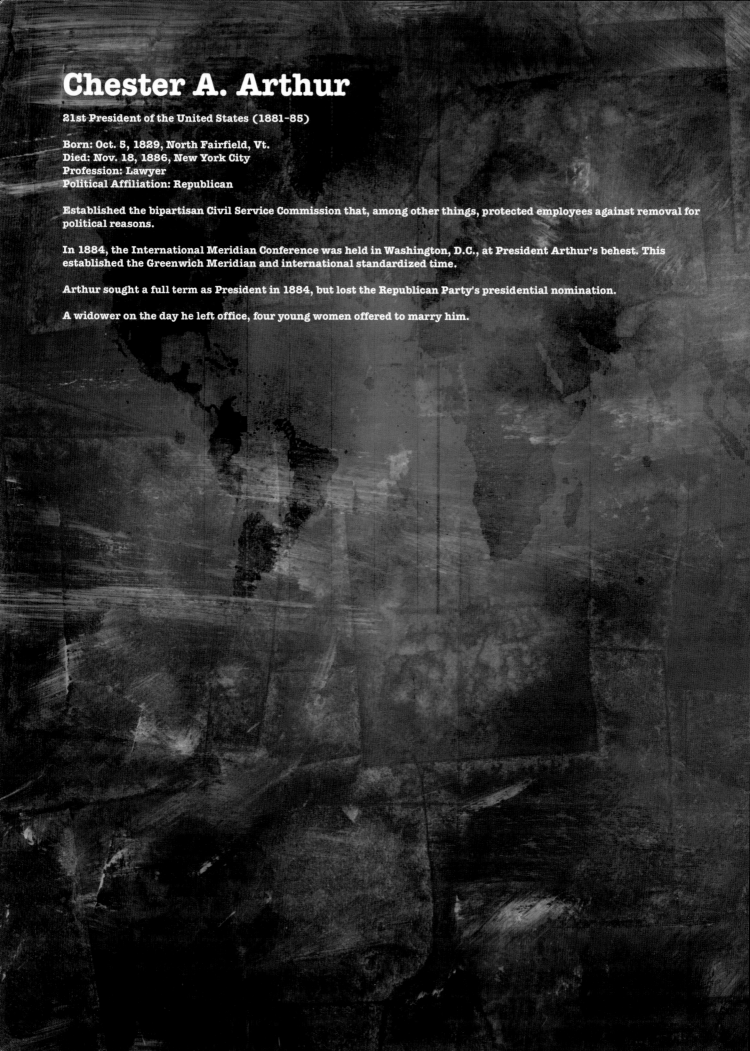

Chester A. Arthur

21st President of the United States (1881-85)

Born: Oct. 5, 1829, North Fairfield, Vt.
Died: Nov. 18, 1886, New York City
Profession: Lawyer
Political Affiliation: Republican

Established the bipartisan Civil Service Commission that, among other things, protected employees against removal for political reasons.

In 1884, the International Meridian Conference was held in Washington, D.C., at President Arthur's behest. This established the Greenwich Meridian and international standardized time.

Arthur sought a full term as President in 1884, but lost the Republican Party's presidential nomination.

A widower on the day he left office, four young women offered to marry him.

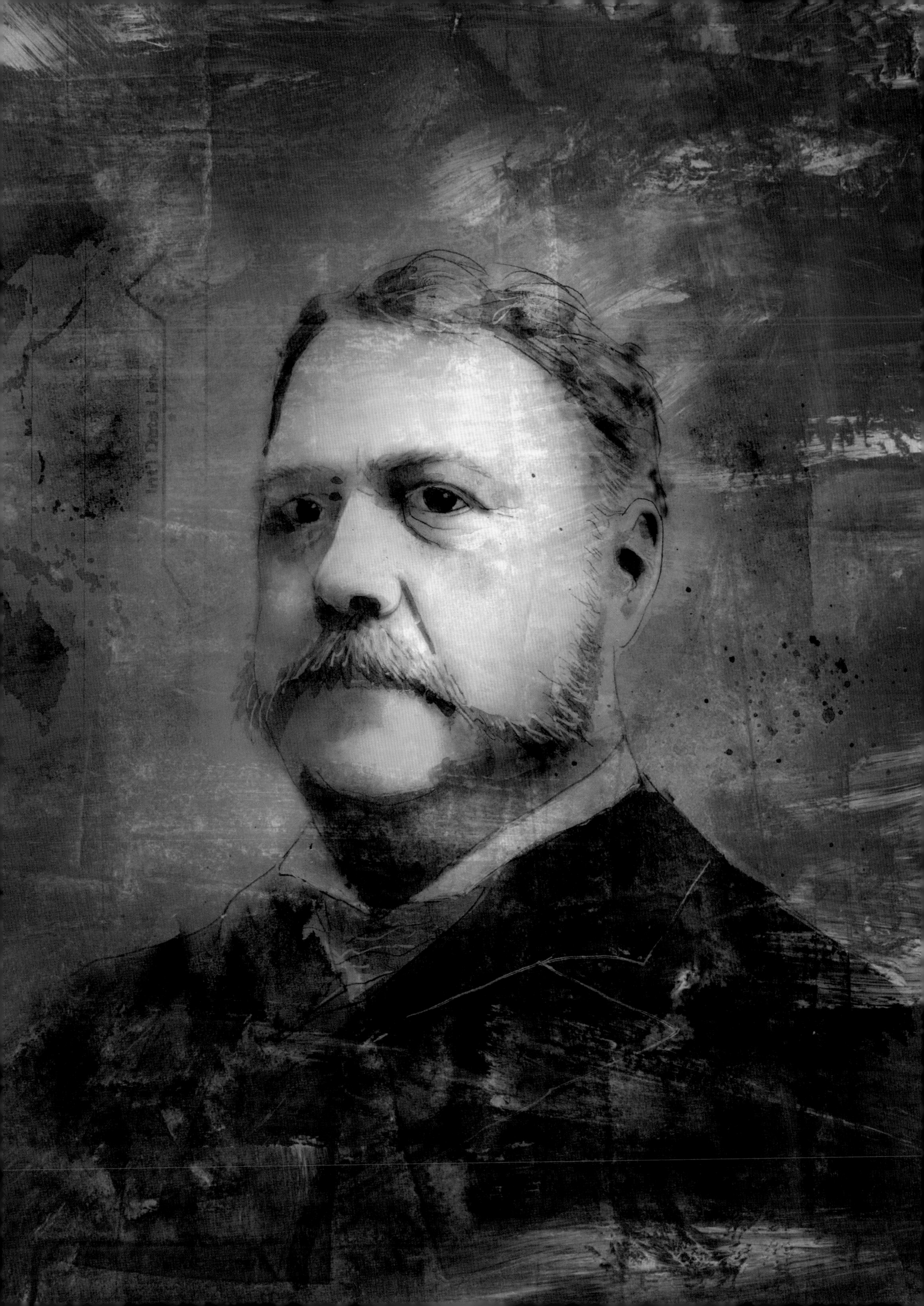

Grover Cleveland

22nd and 24th President of the United States (1885-89, 1893-97)

Born: Mar. 18, 1837, Caldwell, N.J.
Died: June 24, 1908, Princeton, N.J.
Profession: Lawyer
Political Affiliation: Democratic

He vetoed hundreds of private pension bills for American Civil War veterans, believing that their pension requests had already been rejected by the Pensions Bureau. Cleveland used the presidential veto far more than any president up to that time.

One of the most volatile issues of the 1880s was whether the currency should be backed by gold and silver, or by gold alone. Cleveland and Treasury Secretary Daniel Manning stood firmly on the side of the gold standard.

Cleveland was a committed non-interventionist who had campaigned in opposition to expansion and imperialism.

Cleveland entered the White House as a bachelor. On June 2, 1886, Cleveland married Frances Folsom in the Blue Room at the White House. He was the second president to marry while in office, and the only president to wed in the White House.

During the election of 1888 he won the popular vote, but lost the Electoral College vote to Benjamin Harrison. He again contested the presidency in 1892 and won, becoming the only president to serve two non-consecutive terms.

Shortly into Cleveland's second term, the Panic of 1893 struck the stock market and the United States soon faced an acute economic depression.

Helped bring about the end of silver as a basis for American currency.

Cleveland rejected the idea of annexation of Hawaii, where the monarchy had recently been overthrown and a pro-American government installed.

Adopted a broad interpretation of the Monroe Doctrine that did not just simply forbid new European colonies, but declared an American interest in any matter within the hemisphere.

Found to have cancer, Cleveland had surgery performed in secrecy to avoid further panic within the markets in 1893. A cover story about the removal of two bad teeth kept the suspicious press placated.

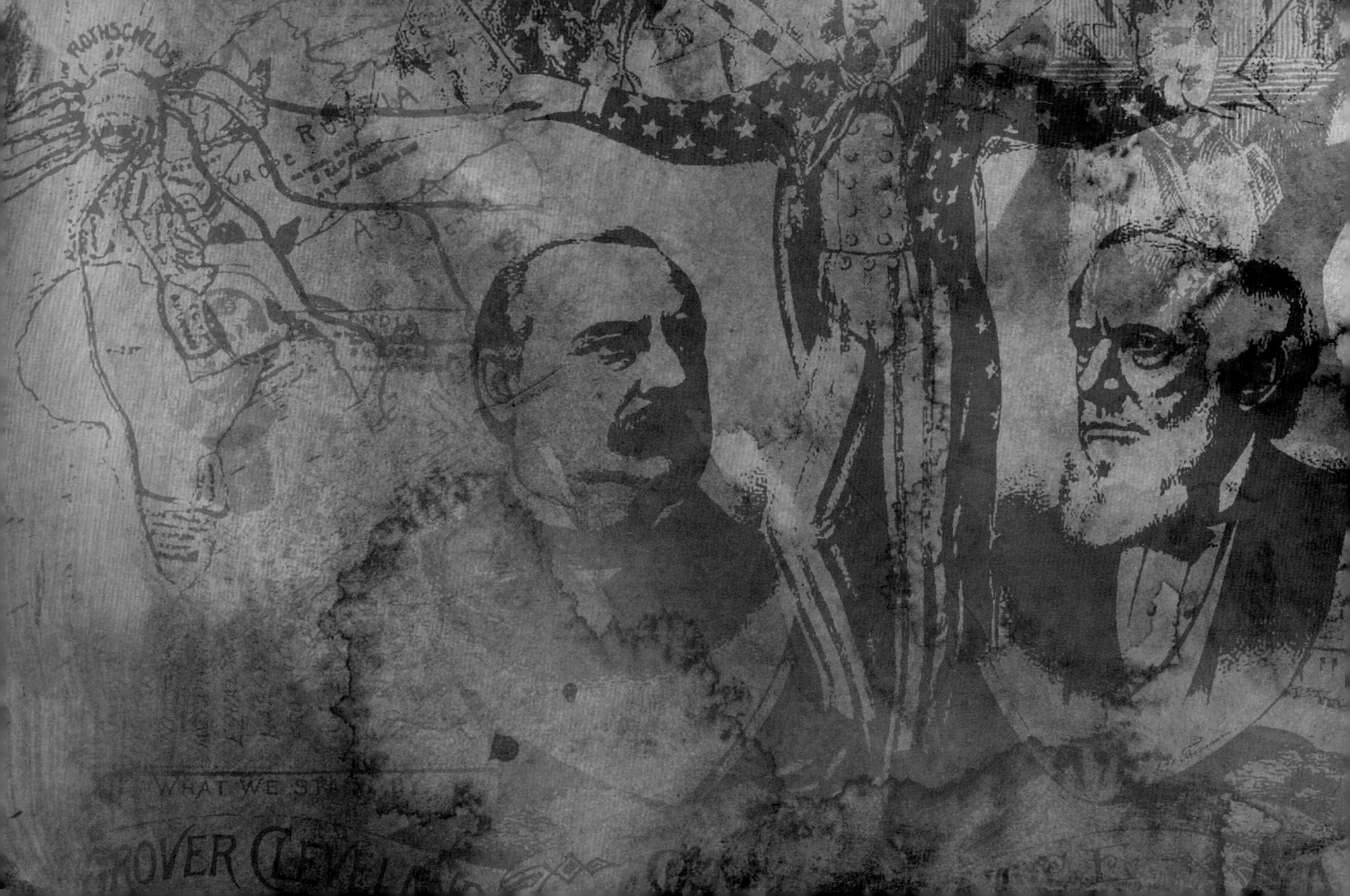
ROTHSCHILDS

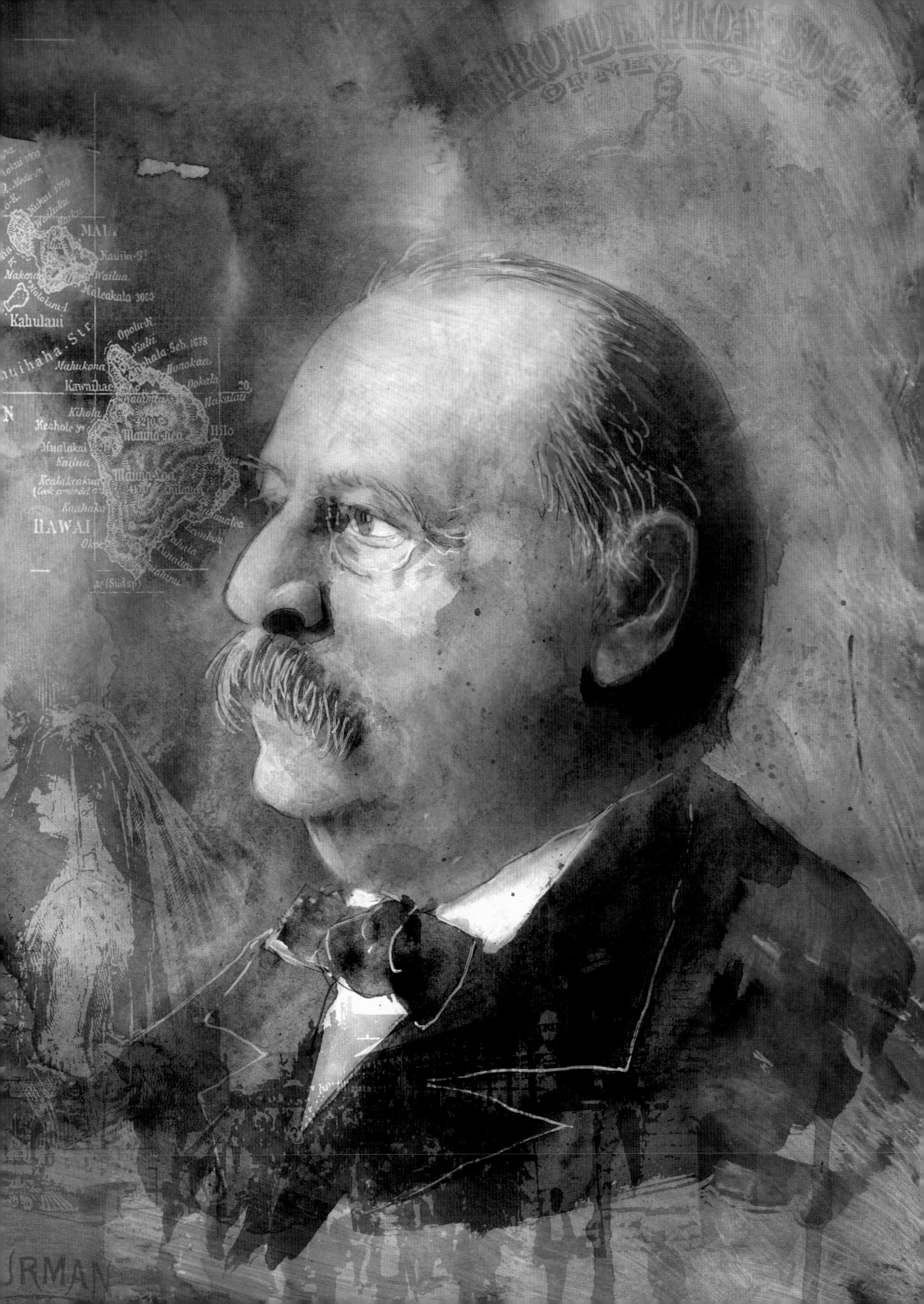
Kahulaui
Wailua
Haleakala 3060
Mahukona
Kawaihae
Honokaa
Ookala
Hakalau
Kiholo
Hilo
Kailua
HAWAI

Benjamin Harrison

23rd President of the United States (1889-93)

Born: Aug. 20, 1833, North Bend, Ohio
Died: Mar. 13, 1901, Indianapolis, Ind.
Profession: Lawyer
Political Affiliation: Republican

Harrison enacted the Dependent and Disability Pension Act in 1890.

The first Pan-American Congress met in Washington, D.C., in 1889, establishing an information center, which later was to become the Pan-American Union.

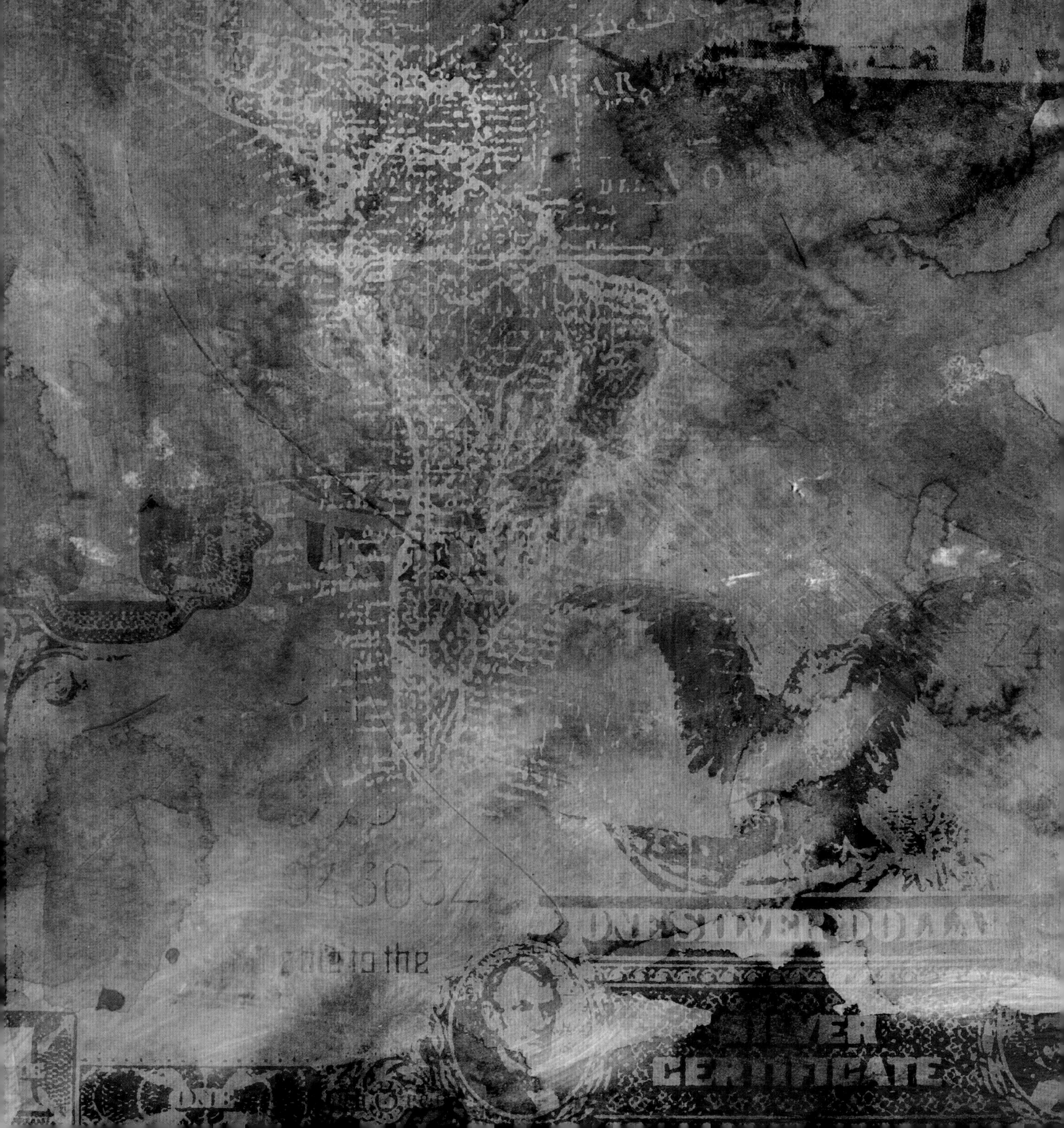

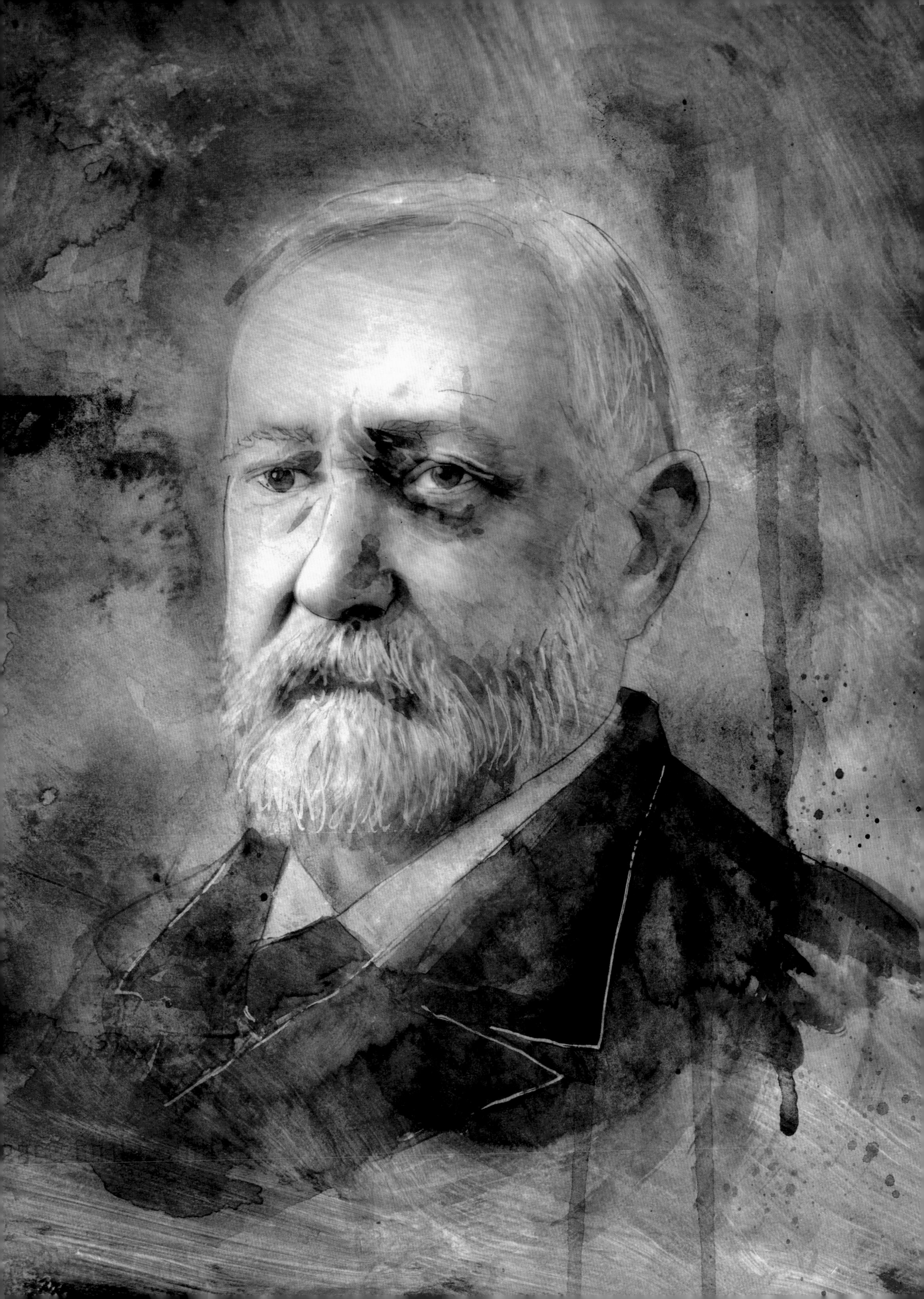

Grover Cleveland

22nd and 24th President of the United States (1885-89, 1893-97)

Born: Mar. 18, 1837, Caldwell, N.J.
Died: June 24, 1908, Princeton, N.J.
Profession: Lawyer
Political Affiliation: Democratic

He vetoed hundreds of private pension bills for American Civil War veterans, believing that their pension requests had already been rejected by the Pensions Bureau. Cleveland used the presidential veto far more than any president up to that time.

One of the most volatile issues of the 1880s was whether the currency should be backed by gold and silver, or by gold alone. Cleveland and Treasury Secretary Daniel Manning stood firmly on the side of the gold standard.

Cleveland was a committed non-interventionist who had campaigned in opposition to expansion and imperialism.

Cleveland entered the White House as a bachelor. On June 2, 1886, Cleveland married Frances Folsom in the Blue Room at the White House. He was the second president to marry while in office, and the only president to wed in the White House.

During the election of 1888 he won the popular vote, but lost the Electoral College vote to Benjamin Harrison. He again contested the presidency in 1892 and won, becoming the only president to serve two non-consecutive terms.

Shortly into Cleveland's second term, the Panic of 1893 struck the stock market and the United States soon faced an acute economic depression.

Helped bring about the end of silver as a basis for American currency.

Cleveland rejected the idea of annexation of Hawaii, where the monarchy had recently been overthrown and a pro-American government installed.

Adopted a broad interpretation of the Monroe Doctrine that did not just simply forbid new European colonies, but declared an American interest in any matter within the hemisphere.

Found to have cancer, Cleveland had surgery performed in secrecy to avoid further panic within the markets in 1893. A cover story about the removal of two bad teeth kept the suspicious press placated.

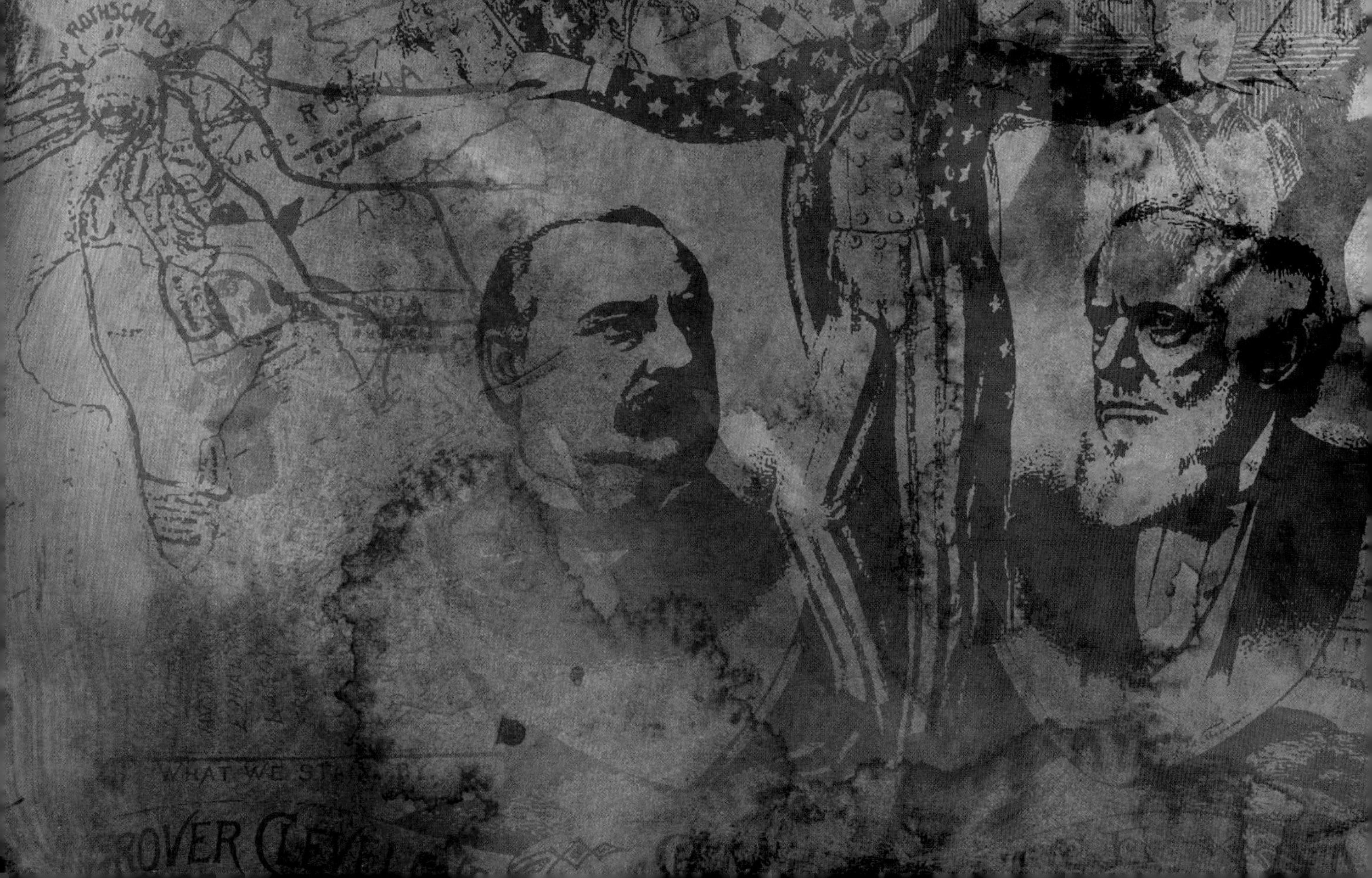

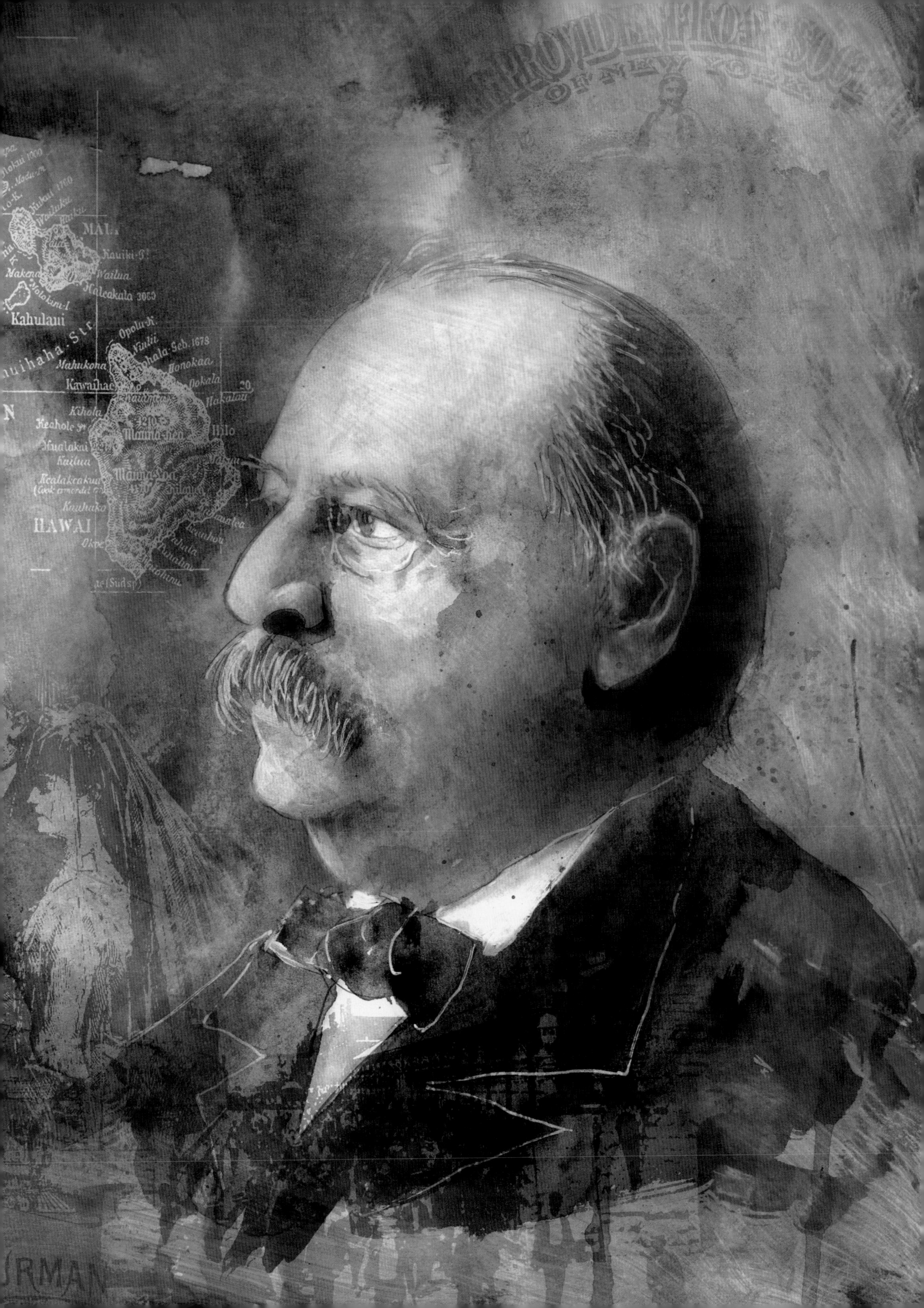

Haleakala 3060
Makena
Wailua
Kahulaui
Mahukona
Kawaihae
Honokaa
Ookala
Kiholo
Hualalai
Kailua
Hilo
Kauhako
HAWAI

William McKinley

25th President of the United States (1897–1901)

Born: Jan. 29, 1843, Niles, Ohio
Died: Sept. 14, 1901, Buffalo, N.Y.
Profession: Lawyer
Political Affiliation: Republican

The first president to campaign by phone.

In 1897, the year McKinley assumed the presidency, there was a substantial revival of business.

On June 16, 1897, a treaty was signed annexing the Republic of Hawaii to the United States.

Rebellions broke out in Cuba, which Spain was unable to contain. In order to protect U.S. interests around Havana, McKinley sent a new warship, the *U.S.S. Maine*, to Havana harbor. On February 15, 1898, the ship mysteriously exploded and sank, causing the deaths of 260 men. Public opinion heated up and Congress authorized war against Spain.

The naval war in Cuba and the Philippines against Spanish interests was a success, becoming the easiest and most profitable war in U.S. history. After 113 days, Spain agreed to peace terms at the Treaty of Paris in July. The United States gained ownership of Guam, the Philippines, and Puerto Rico, and temporary control over Cuba.

On September 6, 1901, Leon Frank Czolgosz, an anarchist, shot McKinley twice while he was attending the Pan-American Exposition. On September 14, he died from gangrene surrounding his wounds. Czolgosz was found guilty of murder and executed in the electric chair.

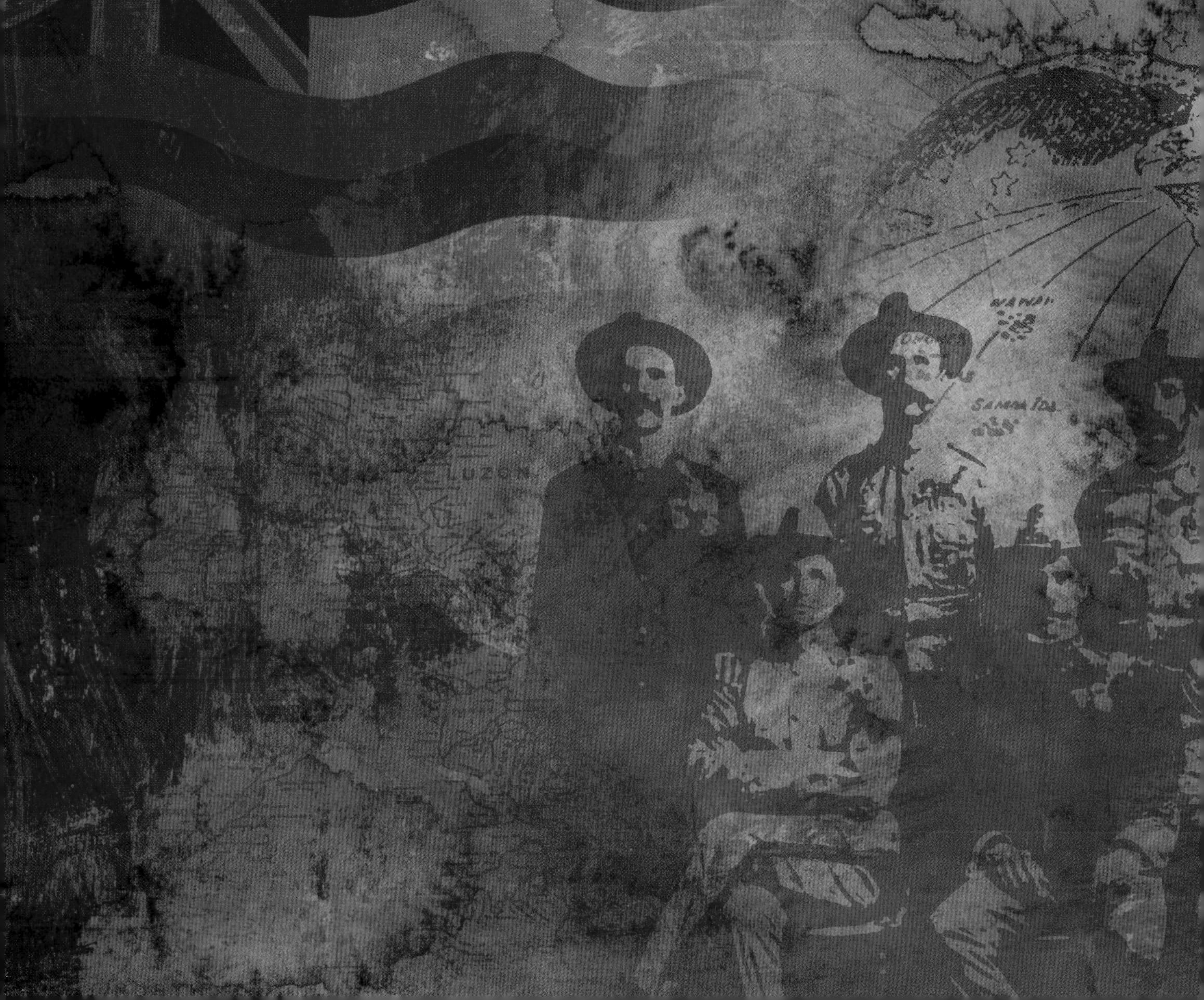
LUZON

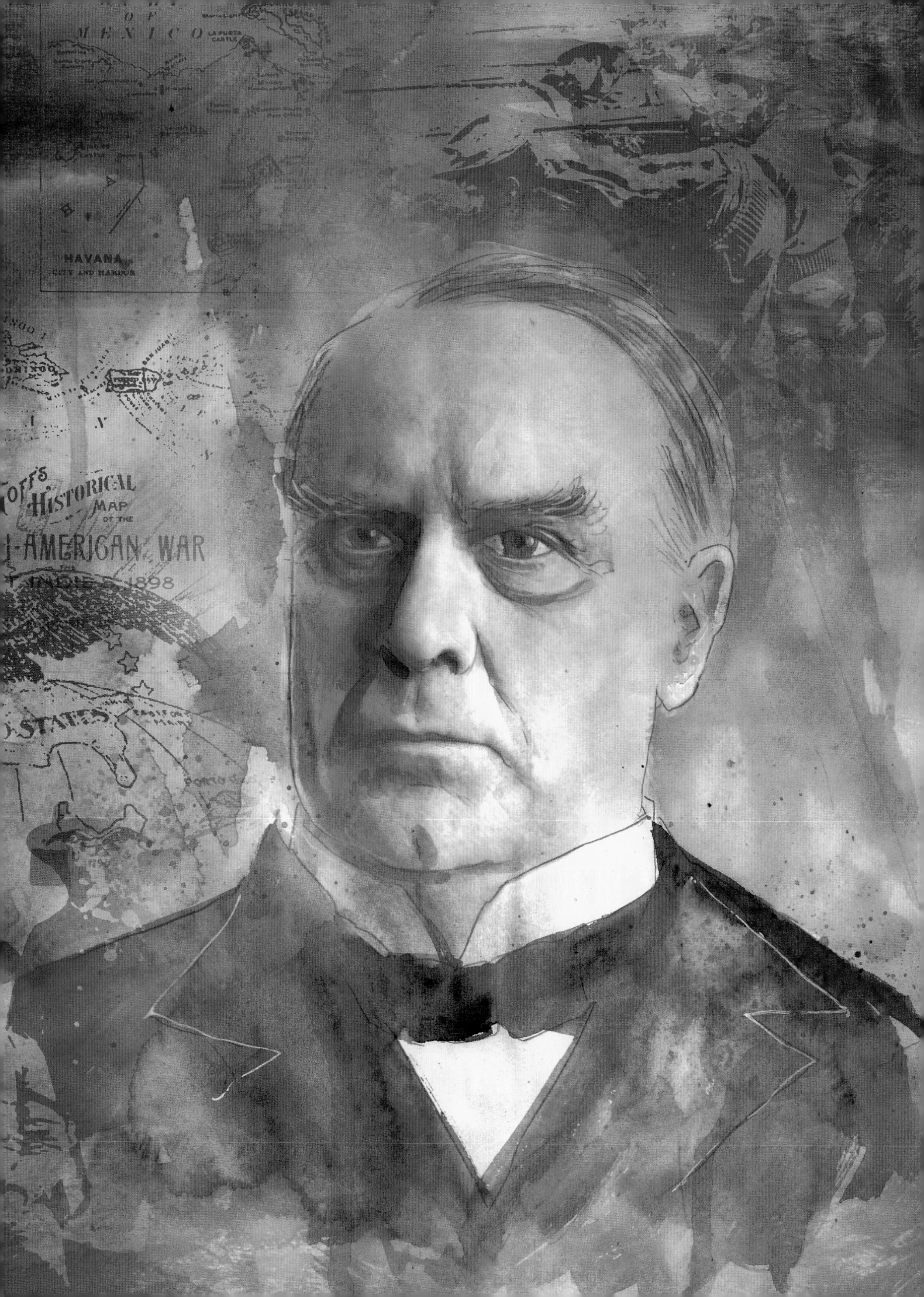
OF MEXICO
HAVANA
CITY AND HARBOR
HISTORICAL
MAP
OF THE
-AMERICAN WAR
1898
STATES

Theodore Roosevelt

26th President of the United States (1901-09)

Born: Oct. 27, 1858, New York City
Died: Jan. 6, 1919, Oyster Bay, N.Y.
Profession: Author, Public Official
Political Affiliation: Republican

A veteran of the war in Cuba, he led his famous "Rough Riders," the First U.S. Volunteer Cavalry Regiment.

When taking the oath of office, Roosevelt did not swear on a bible. He was the youngest person to assume the presidency, at 42.

Issuing 44 lawsuits against major corporations who had formed monopolies, he was called the "trust buster."

Theodore Roosevelt was the fifth vice president to succeed to the office of President, but the first to win election in his own right.

Roosevelt set aside more land for national parks and nature preserves than all of his predecessors combined.

The Philippines saw the U.S. Army for the first time using a systematic doctrine of counter-insurgency.

Roosevelt gained international praise for helping negotiate the end of the Russo-Japanese War, for which he was awarded the Nobel Peace Prize.

Roosevelt's most famous foreign policy initiative, following the Hay-Pauncefote Treaty, was the construction of the Panama Canal.

He dispatched a fleet consisting of four U.S. Navy battleship squadrons, and their escorts, on a worldwide voyage of circumnavigation from December 16, 1907 to February 22, 1909, dubbed "The Great White Fleet" due to their painted white hulls.

He was the first president to travel outside the United States while in office, when he visited Panama.

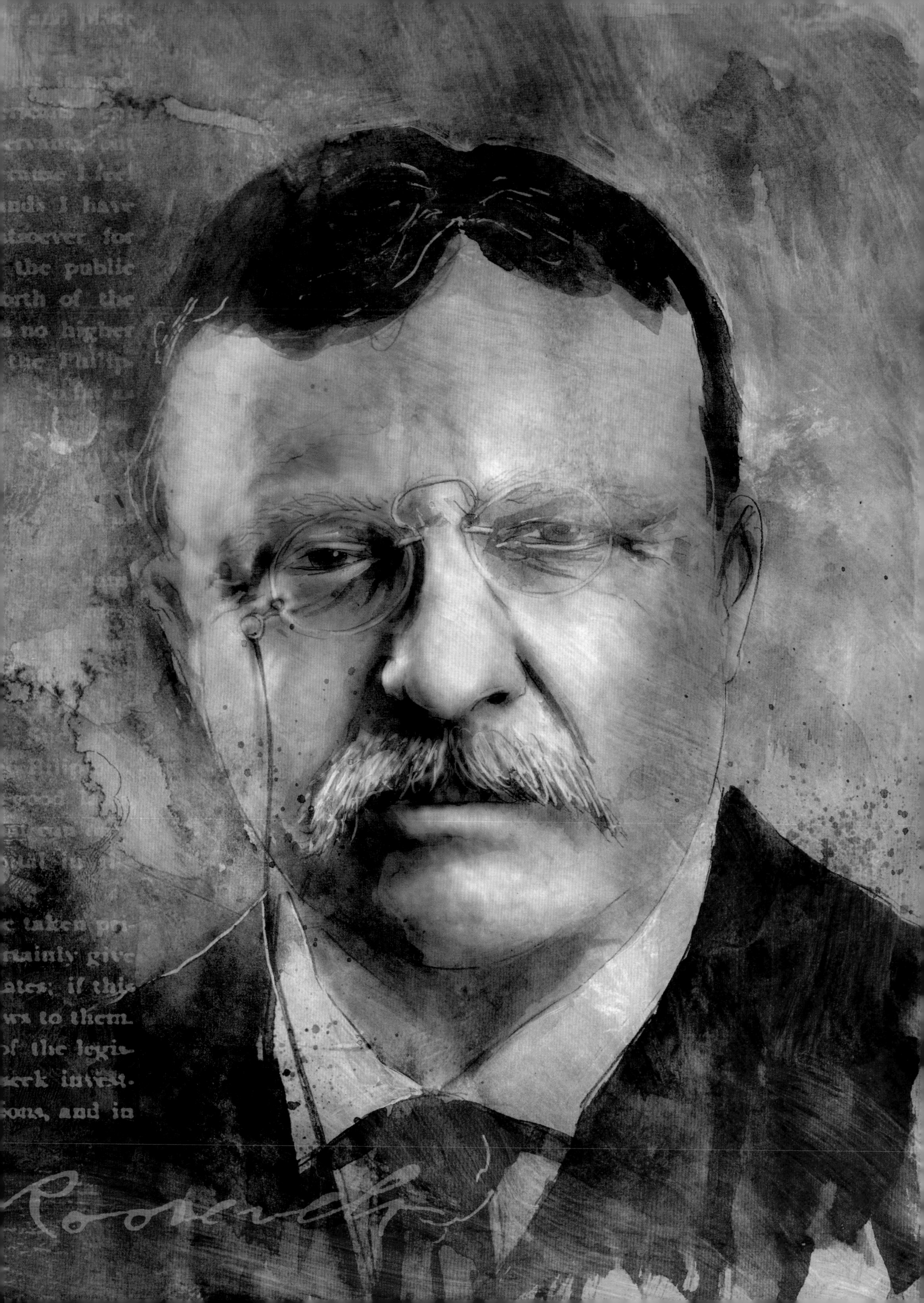

William Howard Taft

27th President of the United States (1909–13)

Born: Sept. 15, 1857, Cincinnati, Ohio
Died: Mar. 8, 1930, Washington, D.C.
Profession: Lawyer, Public Official
Political Affiliation: Republican

Taft fought for the prosecution of trusts, eventually issuing 80 lawsuits and further strengthened the Interstate Commerce Commission.

He supported the 16th Amendment, allowing for a federal income tax, and the 17th Amendment, mandating the direct election of senators by the people.

Taft actively pursued what he termed "Dollar Diplomacy" to further the economic development of less-developed nations of Latin America and Asia through American investment in their infrastructures.

New Mexico and Arizona were both admitted to the Union in 1912.

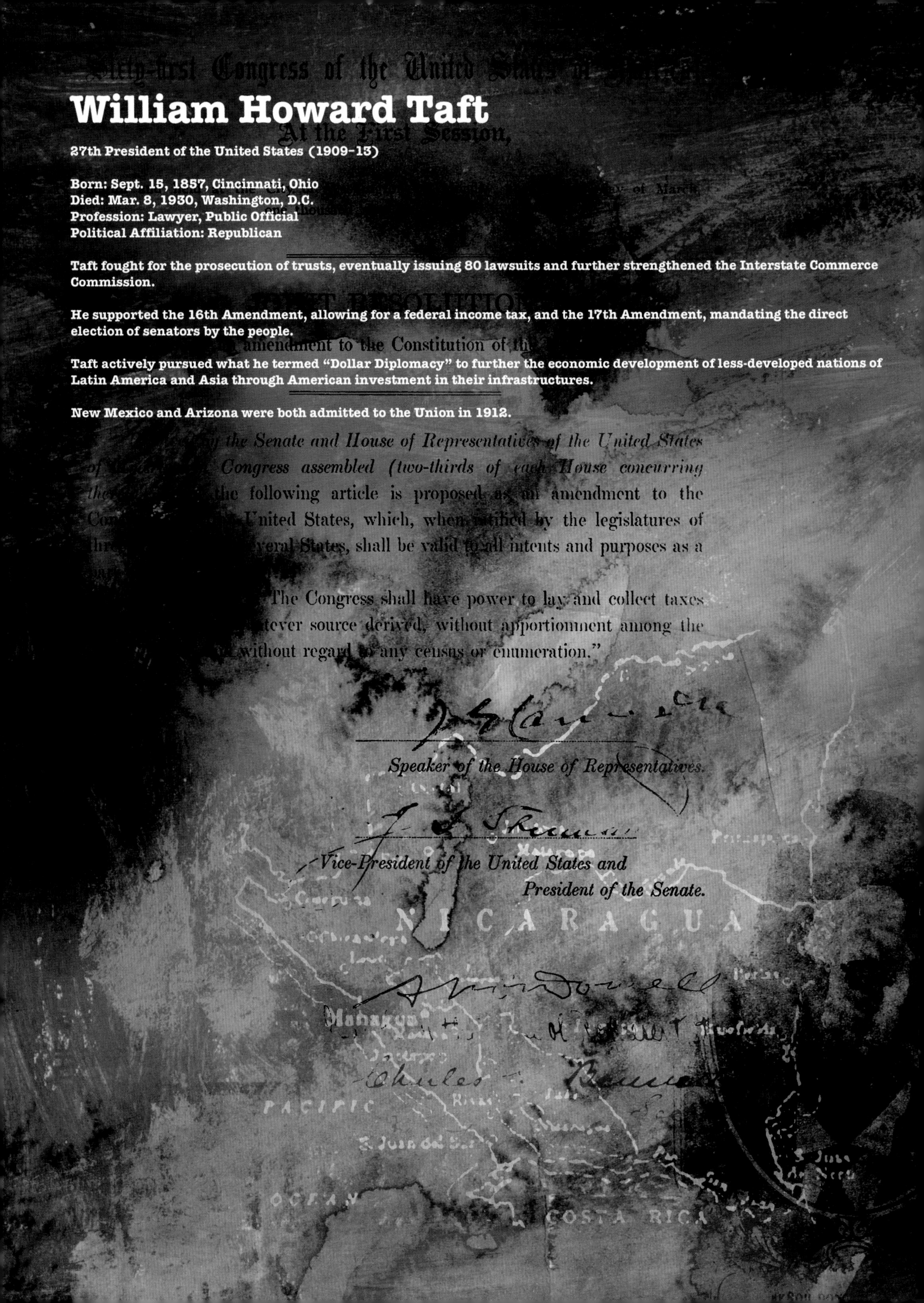

At the First Session,
amendment to the Constitution of
the Senate and House of Representatives of the United States
Congress assembled (two-thirds of each House concurring
the following article is proposed as an amendment to the
United States, which, when ratified by the legislatures of
shall be valid to all intents and purposes as a
The Congress shall have power to lay and collect taxes
source derived, without apportionment among the
without regard to any census or enumeration."
Speaker of the House of Representatives.
Vice-President of the United States and
President of the Senate.
NICARAGUA
PACIFIC
OCEAN
COSTA RICA

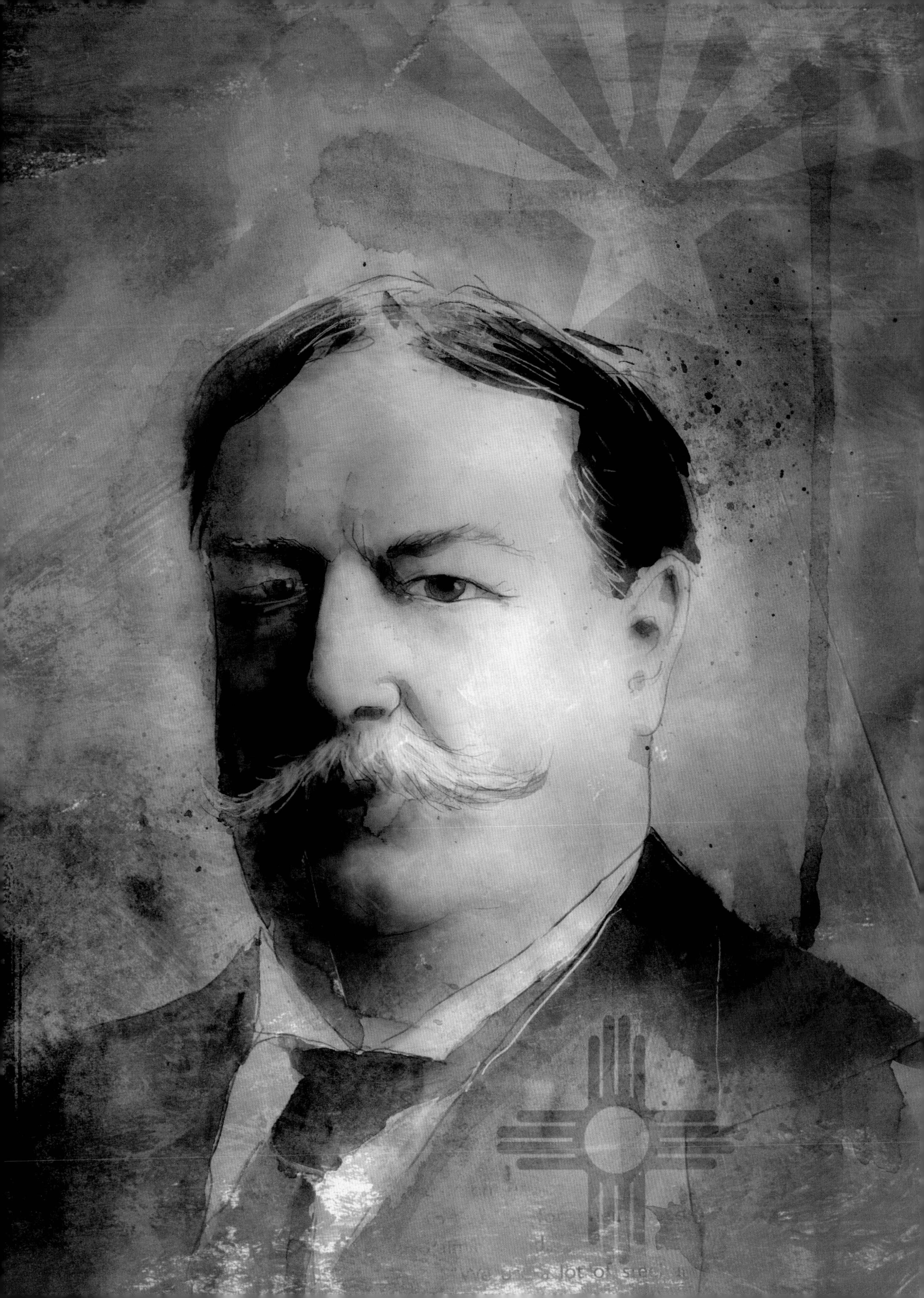

Woodrow Wilson

28th President of the United States (1913-21)

Born: Dec. 28, 1856, Staunton, Va.
Died: Feb. 3, 1924, Washington, D.C.
Profession: Teacher, Public Official
Political Affiliation: Democrat

He held the first modern presidential press conference, on March 15, 1913, in which reporters were allowed to ask him questions.

Wilson was the first Southerner to take office since Andrew Johnson in 1865.

He secured passage of the Federal Reserve System in late 1913 in exchange for campaign support.

Wilson spent 1914 through the beginning of 1917 trying to keep America out of the war in Europe.

Under Wilson, it became accepted policy that "Negro" employees of the Postal Service could have their rank reduced or be dismissed.

U.S. neutrality during World War I would deteriorate when Germany initiated unrestricted submarine warfare in 1917, which threatened U.S. commercial shipping, and when Germany made an attempt to enlist Mexico as an ally. Wilson asked Congress for permission to go to war, and on April 6, 1917, congress officially declared it.

He pushed the Espionage Act of 1917 and the Sedition Act of 1918 through Congress to suppress anti-British, pro-German, or anti-war opinions.

The American Protective League was a quasi-private organization with 250,000 members in 600 cities, sanctioned by the Wilson administration. These men carried Government Issue badges and freely conducted warrantless searches and interrogations.

Wilson's "14 Points" were the only war aims clearly expressed by any belligerent nation during the war, and thus became the basis for the Treaty of Versailles following World War I, and called for the formation of the League of Nations.

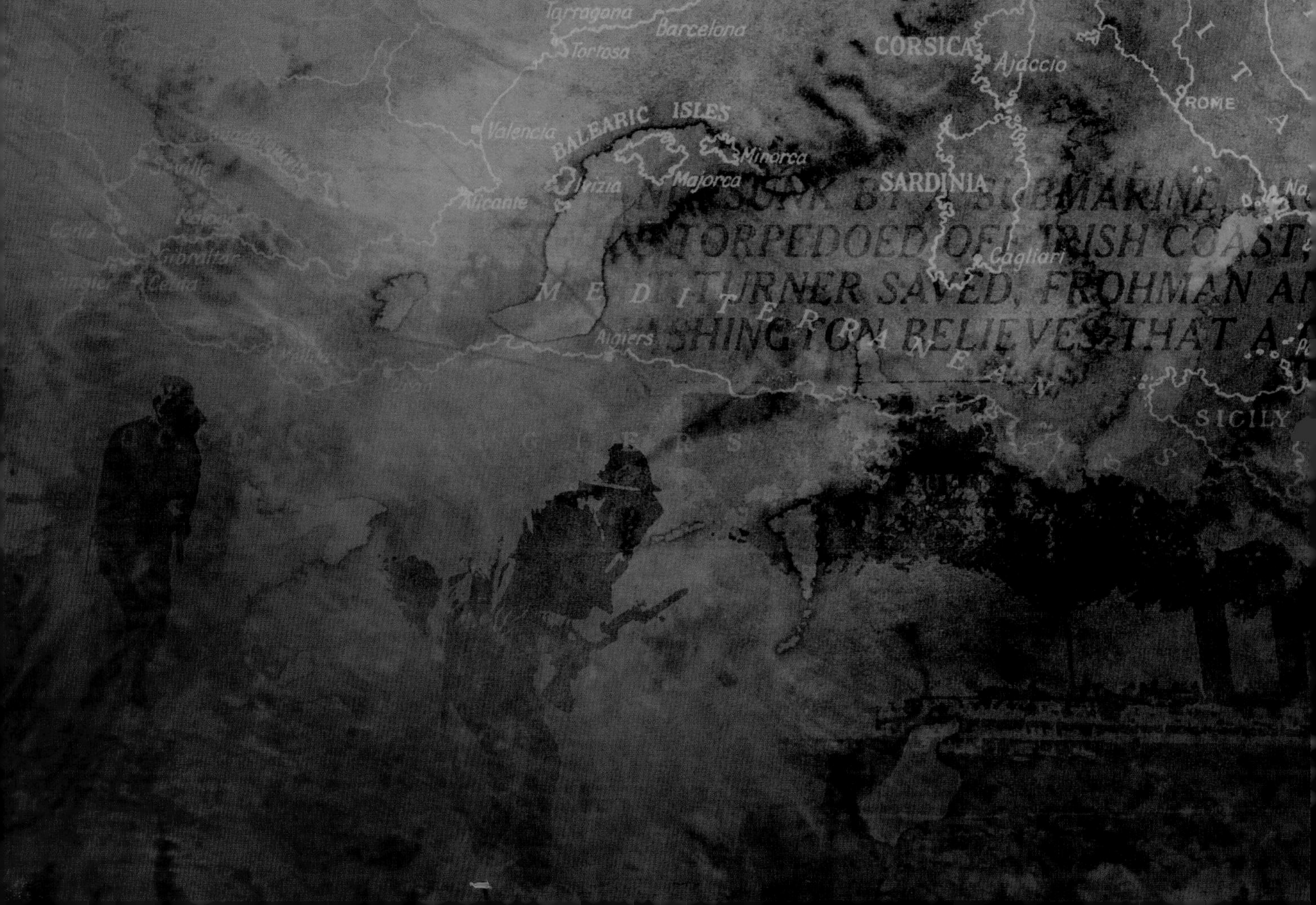
Tarragona
Barcelona
Tortosa
CORSICA
Ajaccio
ROME
BALEARIC ISLES
Valencia
Minorca
Majorca
Alicante
SARDINIA
TORPEDOED OFF IRISH COAST
Cagliari
SICILY

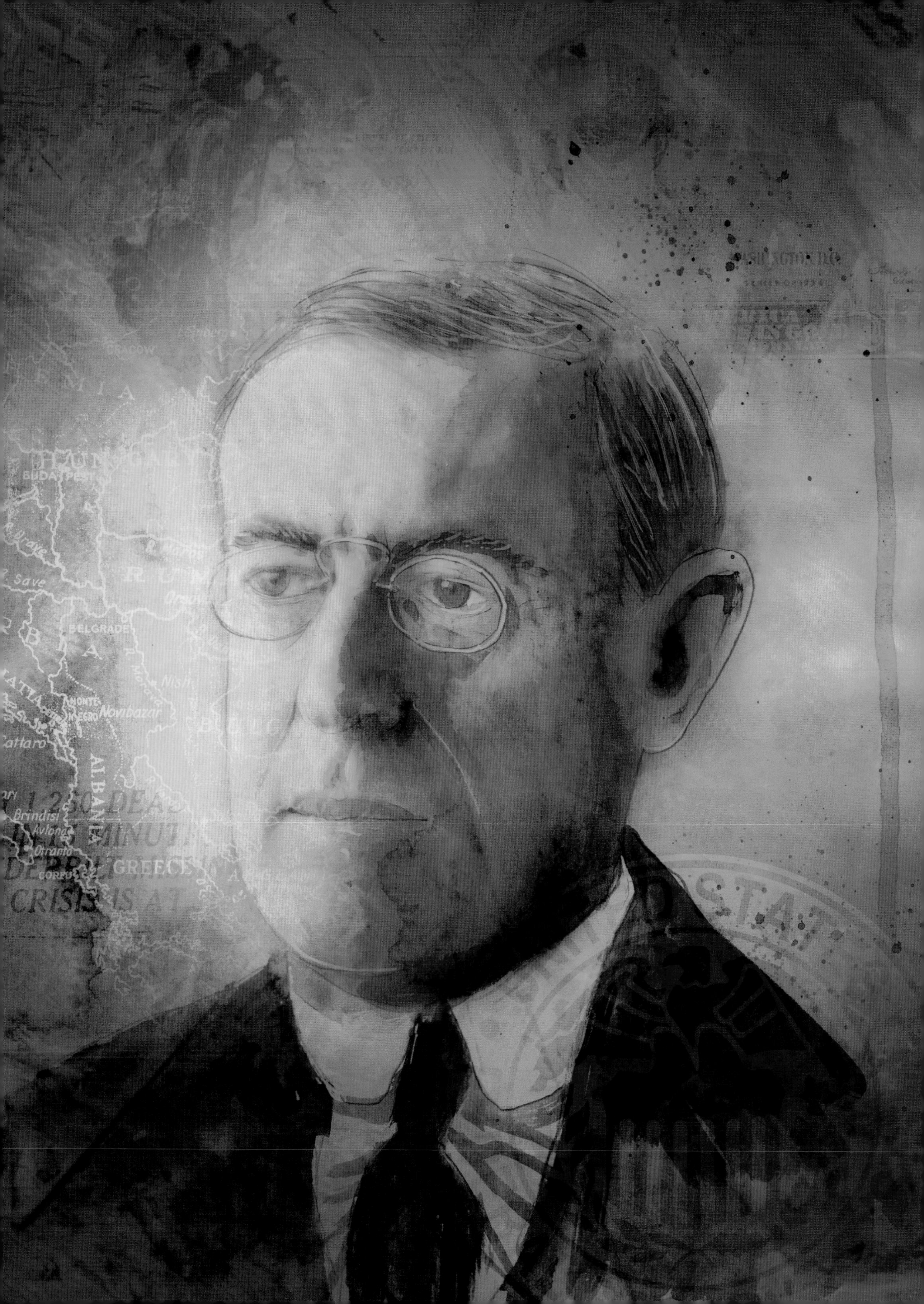
CRACOW
BUDAPEST
Save
BELGRADE
Nish
Novibazar
Cattaro
ALBANIA
Brindisi
Avlona
Otranto
CORFU
GREECE
CRISIS IS AT

Warren G. Harding

29th President of the United States (1921-23)

Born: Nov. 2, 1865, Corsica (now Blooming Grove), Ohio
Died: Aug. 2, 1923, San Francisco, Calif.
Profession: Editor-Publisher
Political Affiliation: Republican

Harding pushed for the establishment of the Bureau of Veterans Affairs, later organized as the Department of Veterans Affairs.

He signed peace treaties with Germany, Austria, and Hungary, formally ending World War I for the United States.

His administration was beset by many scandals and corruption.

He became the first president to visit Alaska.

Harding died of either a heart attack or a stroke on August 2, 1923. He had been ill for one week.

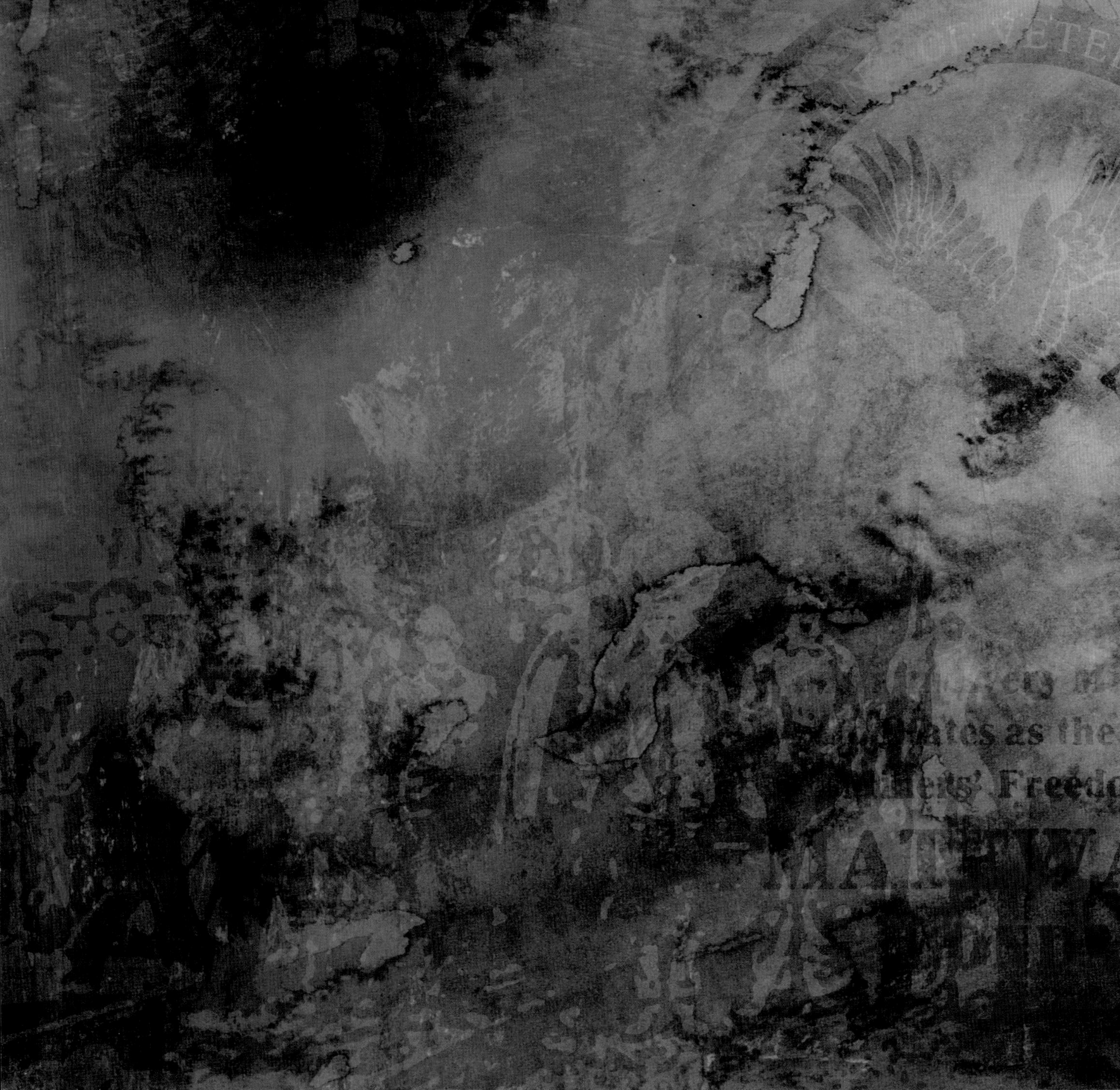

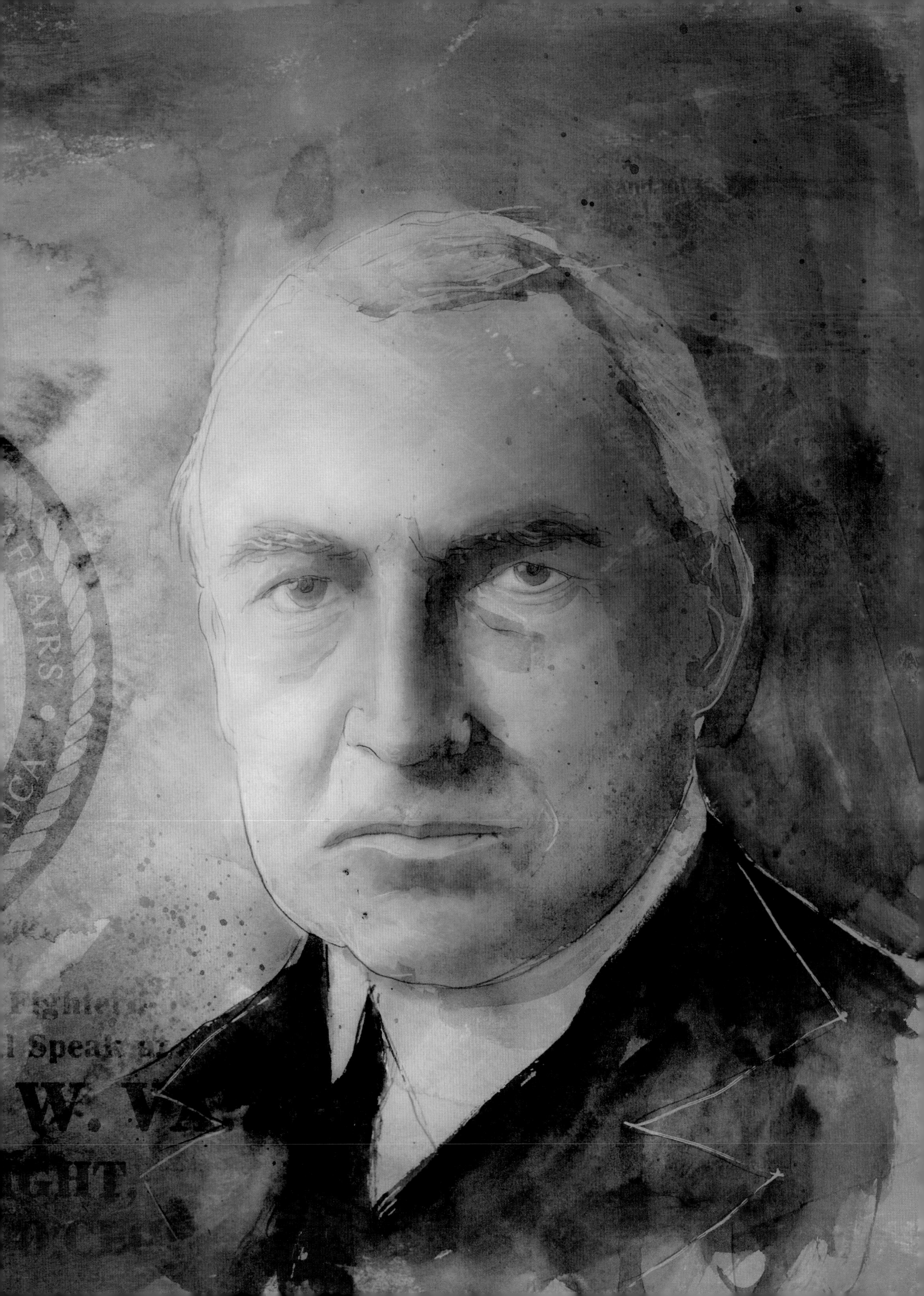

Calvin Coolidge

30th President of the United States (1923-29)

Born: July 4, 1872, Plymouth Notch, Vt.
Died: Jan. 5, 1933, Northampton, Mass.
Profession: Lawyer
Political Affiliation: Republican

When President Harding died while on a speaking tour in California, Vice President Coolidge was visiting his family home in Vermont, which did not have electricity or a telephone. He received word by messenger of Harding's death.

Shortly after the Republican convention of 1924, where he was nominated as their Presidential candidate, Coolidge's son died from an infected blister. He went on to win the election.

Coolidge has often been criticized for his lack of action during the Great Mississippi Flood of 1927, the worst natural disaster to hit the Gulf Coast until Hurricane Katrina in 2005.

Coolidge continued the previous administration's policy of not recognizing the newly formed Soviet Union.

He made himself available to reporters, giving 529 press conferences, meeting with reporters more regularly than any President before or since.

Coolidge chose to not seek renomination for President in 1928.

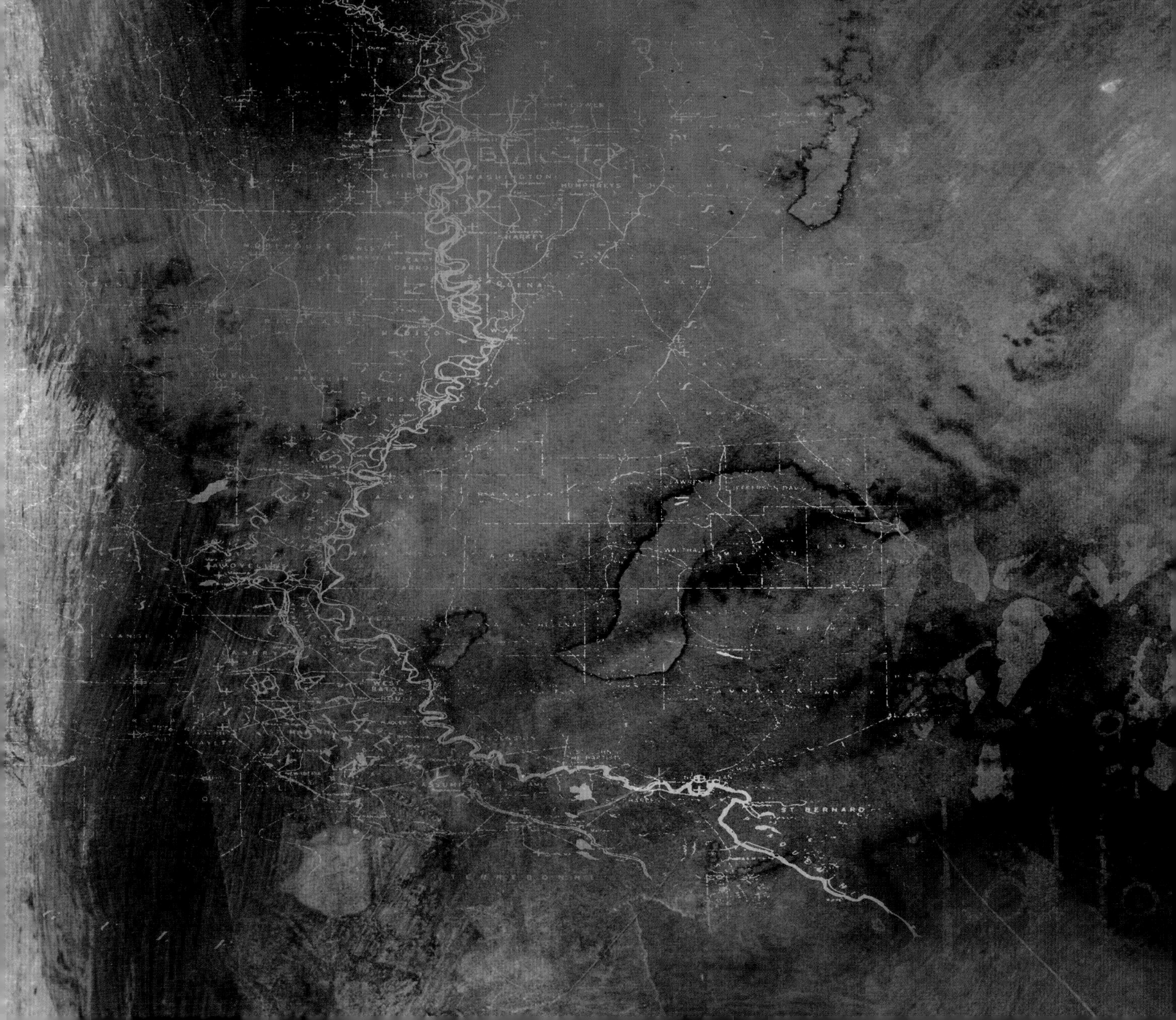
ST BERNARD

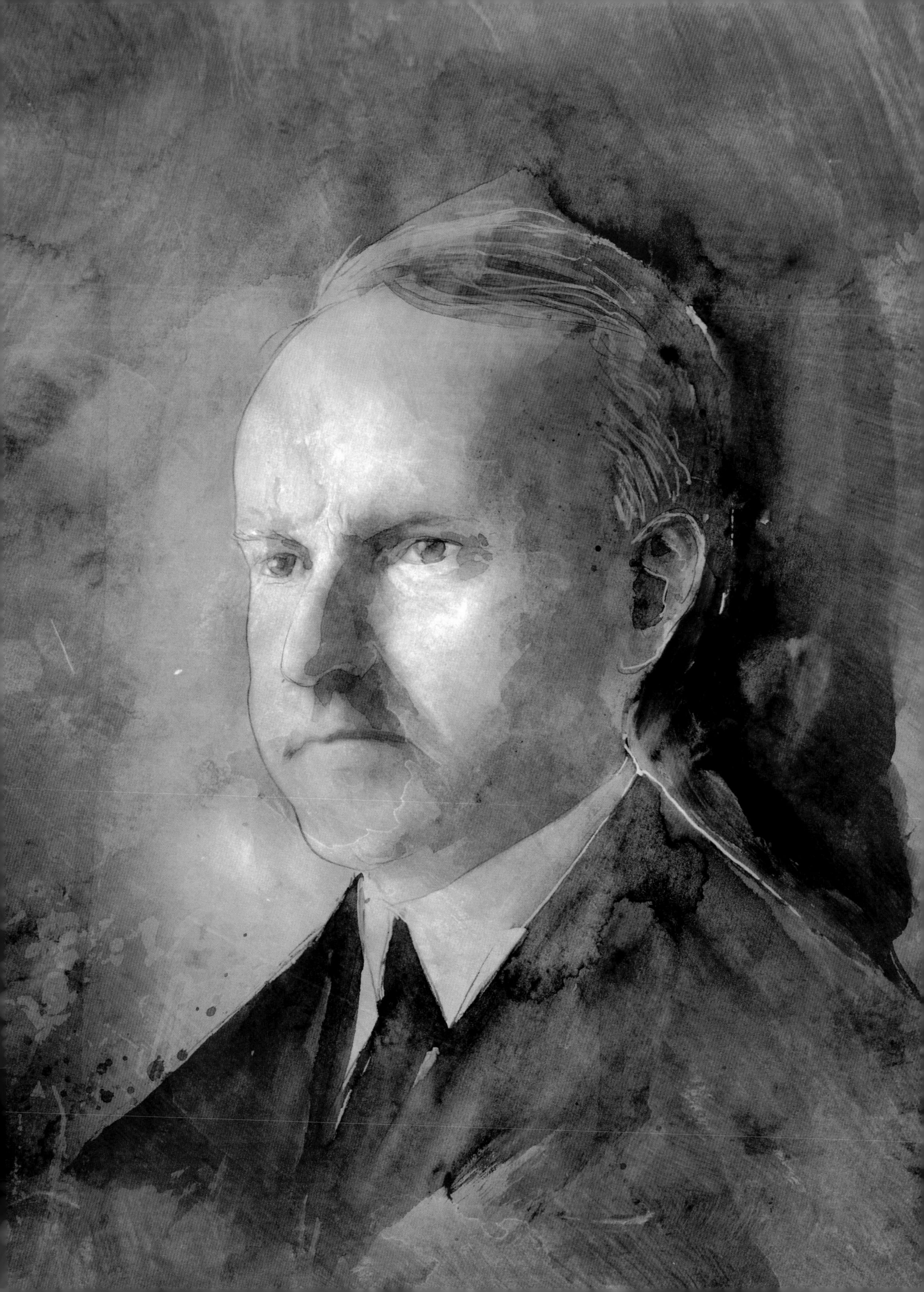

Herbert Hoover

31st President of the United States (1929-33)

Born: Aug. 10, 1874, West Branch, Iowa
Died: Oct. 20, 1964, New York City
Profession: Engineer
Political Affiliation: Republican

Hoover instructed the Justice Department and the Internal Revenue Service to go after gangsters for tax evasion. He enabled the prosecution of gangster Al Capone.

While in Argentina as part of a goodwill tour, he escaped an assassination attempt by Argentine anarchists led by Severino Di Giovanni, who attempted to blow up the railroad car in which he was travelling.

On October 29, 1929, the stock market crashed, marking the beginning of the Great Depression. This date is known as Black Tuesday.

Hoover made attempts to stop "the downward spiral" of the Great Depression. His policies, however, had little or no effect. He declined to pursue legislative relief, believing that it would make people dependent on the federal government.

Authorized the Mexican Repatriation program designed to combat rampant unemployment and remove people seen as usurpers of American jobs. The program was largely a forced migration of an estimated 500,000 Mexicans and Mexican Americans to Mexico. The program continued until 1937.

By 1932, the Great Depression had spread across the globe. In the United States, unemployment had reached 24.9%. More than 5,000 banks failed and tens of thousands of shantytowns and tent cities began to appear. They became known as "Hoover-villes."

The Revenue Act of 1932 raised income tax on the highest incomes from 25% to 63%. The estate tax was doubled and corporate taxes were raised by almost 15%.

The final attempt of the Hoover Administration to rescue the economy was the passage of the Emergency Relief and Construction Act, which included funds for public works programs and the creation of the Reconstruction Finance Corporation (RFC) in 1932. It was later adopted by Franklin Delano Roosevelt and greatly expanded as part of his New Deal.

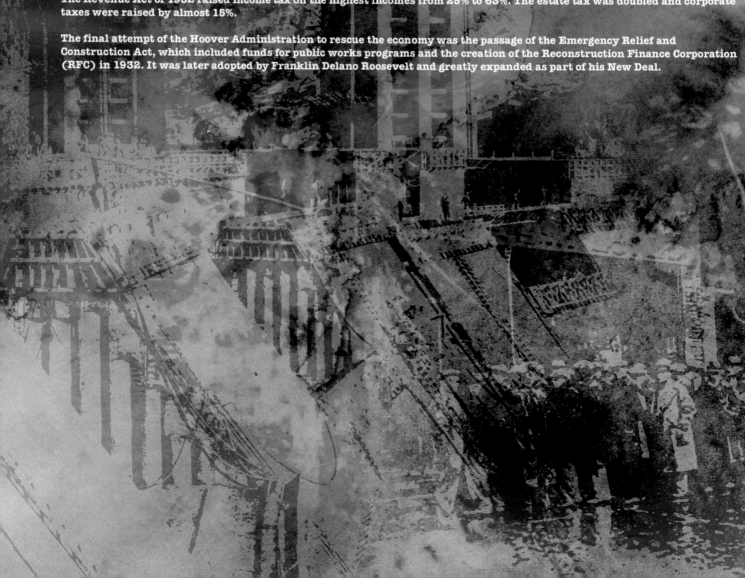

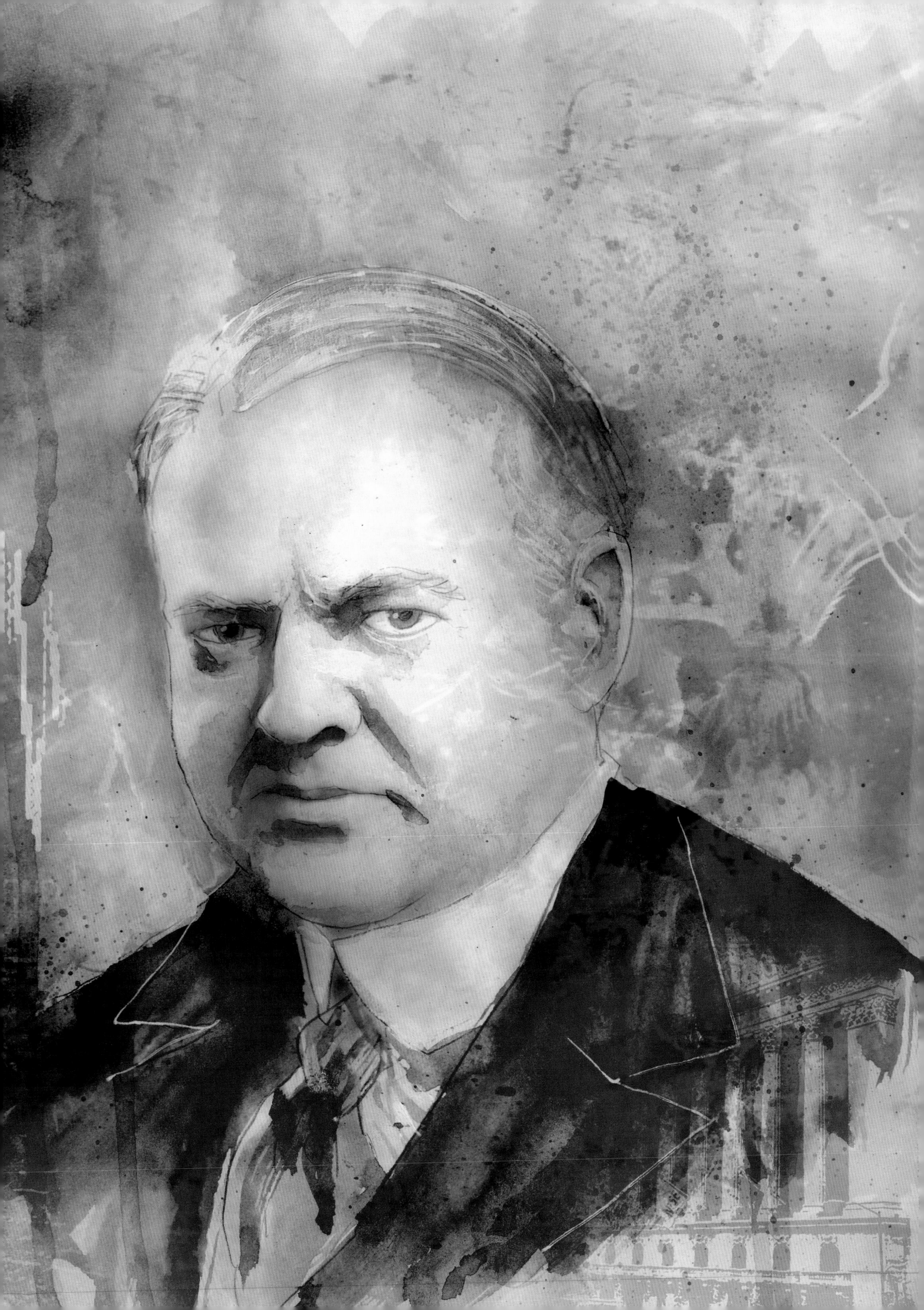

Franklin Delano Roosevelt

32nd President of the United States (1933-45)

Born: Jan. 30, 1882, Hyde Park, N.Y.
Died: Apr. 12, 1945, Warm Springs, Ga.
Profession: Lawyer, Public Official
Political Affiliation: Democrat

Roosevelt's inauguration on March 4, 1933 occurred in the middle of a bank panic.

From March 9 to June 16, 1933, he sent Congress a record number of bills, all of which passed easily as he enacted his "New Deal."

In a controversial move, Roosevelt gave Executive Order 6102, which made all privately held gold of American citizens property of the U.S. Treasury. Gold bullion remained illegal for Americans to own until 1974.

Roosevelt also kept his promise to push for repeal of Prohibition. In April 1933, he issued an Executive Order redefining 3.2% alcohol as the maximum allowed.

The Social Security Act established Social Security and promised economic security for the elderly, the poor, and the sick.

The economy grew 58% from 1932 to 1940 in eight years of peace, and then grew 56% from 1940 to 1945 in five years of wartime.

In 1935, at the time of Italy's invasion of Ethiopia, and as Hitler rose in Germany, Congress passed the Neutrality Act, applying a mandatory ban on the shipment of arms from the United States to any combatant nation.

When World War II broke out in 1939, Roosevelt rejected the Wilson neutrality stance and sought ways to assist Britain and France militarily.

After the fall of Paris to Nazi Germany, isolationist sentiments declined in the United States. Roosevelt successfully urged Congress to enact the first peacetime draft in U.S. history in 1940 and rapidly expanded the military.

In 1940, Roosevelt broke with tradition, ran, and won a third consecutive presidential term. He would go on to win a fourth.

By mid-1941, Roosevelt had committed the U.S. to the Allied side of the war with a policy of "all aid short of war."

On December 7, 1941, the Japanese attacked the U.S. Pacific Fleet at Pearl Harbor, destroying or damaging 16 warships, including most of the fleet's battleships, and killing more than 2,400 American military personnel and civilians. On December 11, Germany and Italy declared war on the United States.

Roosevelt signed Executive Order 9066, which imprisoned thousands of Japanese Americans.

Roosevelt, only 62 in 1944, had been in declining health since at least 1940. He went on to win the 1944 election. On April 12, 1945, he died of a stroke. Less than a month after his death, on May 8, Germany surrendered.

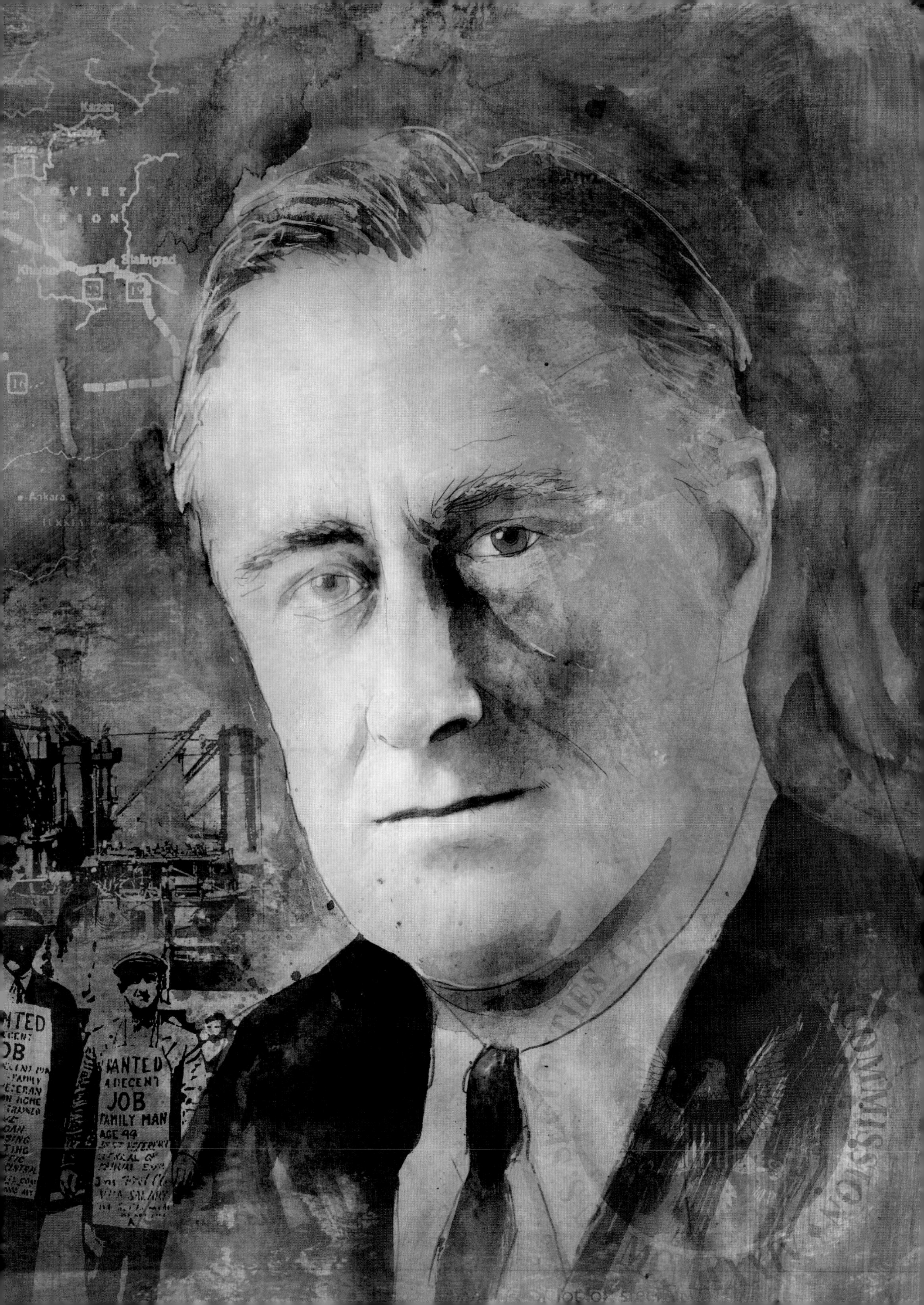

Kazan
Stalingrad
Ankara
WANTED
A DECENT
JOB
FAMILY MAN
AGE 44
COMMISSION

Harry S. Truman

33rd President of the United States (1945-53)

Born: May 8, 1884, Lamar, Mo.
Died: Dec. 26, 1972, Kansas City, Mo.
Profession: Farmer, Public Official
Political Affiliation: Democrat

Truman had been vice president for only 82 days when Roosevelt died and he assumed the presidency.

Truman was quickly briefed on the Manhattan Project and gave authorization for the use of atomic weapons against the Japanese in August 1945, after Japan refused to surrender under the Potsdam Declaration. The atomic bombings of Hiroshima and Nagasaki that followed were the first, and so far the only, instance of nuclear warfare. The Japanese agreed to surrender on August 14.

As the economy switched back to a peacetime footing, there was a wave of destabilizing strikes in major industries.

Truman strongly supported the creation of the United Nations. Under the National Security Act of 1947 he merged the Department of War and the Department of the Navy into the National Military Establishment, later the Department of Defence, and created the U.S. Air Force. The act also created the CIA and the National Security Council.

He was able to win bipartisan support for both the Truman Doctrine, which formalized a policy of containment of the Soviets, and the Marshall Plan, which aimed to help rebuild post-war Europe.

Truman recognized the State of Israel on May 14, 1948, eleven minutes after it declared itself a nation.

He approved the Berlin Airlift, a campaign that delivered food and other supplies such as coal to a blockaded West Berlin, using military airplanes on a massive scale.

Truman had proposed disbanding the Marine Corps as part of the 1948 defence reorganization plan.

He won what was perceived by the press as an un-winnable election in 1948.

Truman was a strong supporter of the North Atlantic Treaty Organization (NATO), which established a formal peacetime military alliance with Canada and many of the democratic European nations that had not fallen under Soviet control following World War II.

President Truman recognized the newly created state of Pakistan in 1947, making the United States one of the first countries in the world to do so.

On June 25, 1950, North Korea invaded South Korea. The UN authorized armed defence for the first time in its history.

Concerned his actions in the Korean War could bring the Soviet Union into the conflict, Truman fired General MacArthur from all his commands in Korea and Japan. Truman's approval ratings plummeted, and he faced calls for his impeachment.

The war remained a frustrating stalemate for two years, with over 30,000 Americans killed, until a peace agreement restored borders and ended the conflict.

On November 1, 1950, Puerto Rican nationalists Griselio Torresola and Oscar Collazo attempted to assassinate Truman at Blair House.

In 1951, the United States ratified the 22nd Amendment, making a president ineligible to be elected for a third time, or to be elected for a second time after having served more than two years of a previous president's term. Truman was, however, grandfathered in but decided not to run for re-election.

When he left office in 1953, Truman was one of the most unpopular chief executives in history.

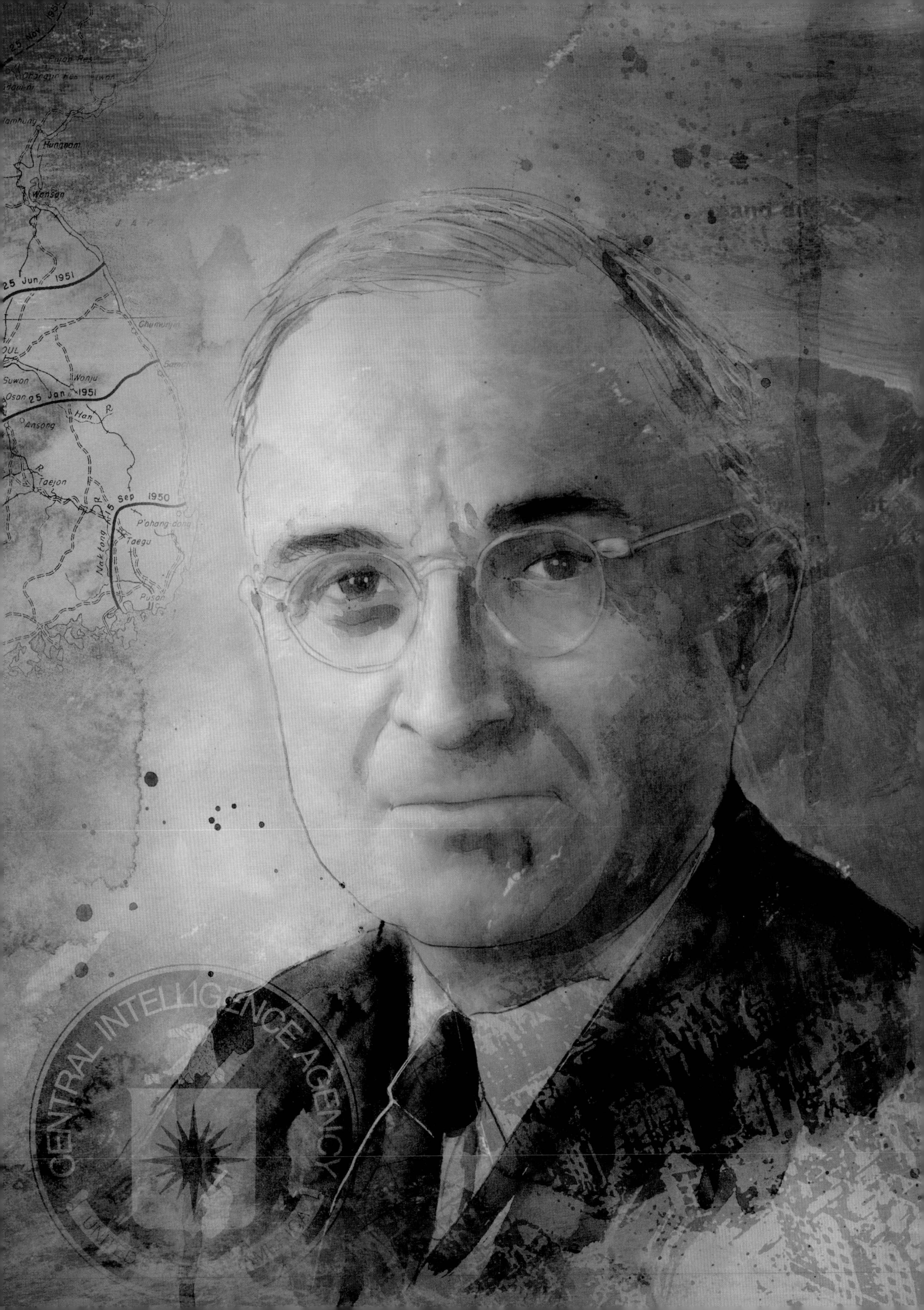
Hungnam
Wonsan
25 Jun 1951
Chumunjin
Suwon
Wonju
Osan
25 Jan 1951
Han R
Ansong
Taejon
15 Sep 1950
P'ohang-dong
Taegu
Naktong R
Pusan
CENTRAL INTELLIGENCE AGENCY

Dwight D. Eisenhower

34th President of the United States (1953-61)

Born: Oct. 14, 1890, Denison, Tex.
Died: Mar. 28, 1969, Washington, D.C.
Profession: Soldier
Political Affiliation: Republican

Eisenhower authorized the Interstate Highway System with the Federal Aid Highway Act of 1956.

After the Suez Crisis, the United States became the protector of most Western interests in the Middle East. As a result, Eisenhower proclaimed the "Eisenhower Doctrine" in January 1957.

Eisenhower explored the option of supporting the French colonial forces in Vietnam who were fighting an independence insurrection there. However, Chief of Staff Matthew Ridgway dissuaded the president from intervening by presenting a comprehensive estimate of the massive military deployment that would be necessary.

He supported the 1954 Brown v. Board of Education of Topeka U.S. Supreme Court decision, in which segregated ("separate but equal") schools were ruled to be unconstitutional. The "Little Rock Nine" incident of 1957 involved the refusal by Arkansas to honor a Federal court order to integrate the schools. Under Executive Order 10730, Eisenhower placed the Arkansas National Guard under federal control and sent Army troops to escort nine black students into an all-white public school.

In 1961, Eisenhower became the first U.S. president to be "constitutionally forced" from office, having served the maximum two terms allowed by the 22nd Amendment to the U.S. Constitution.

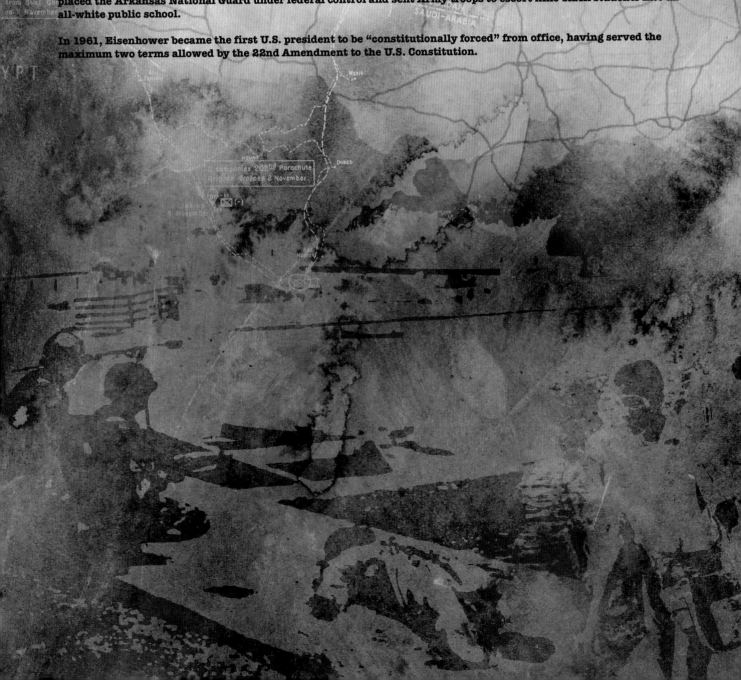

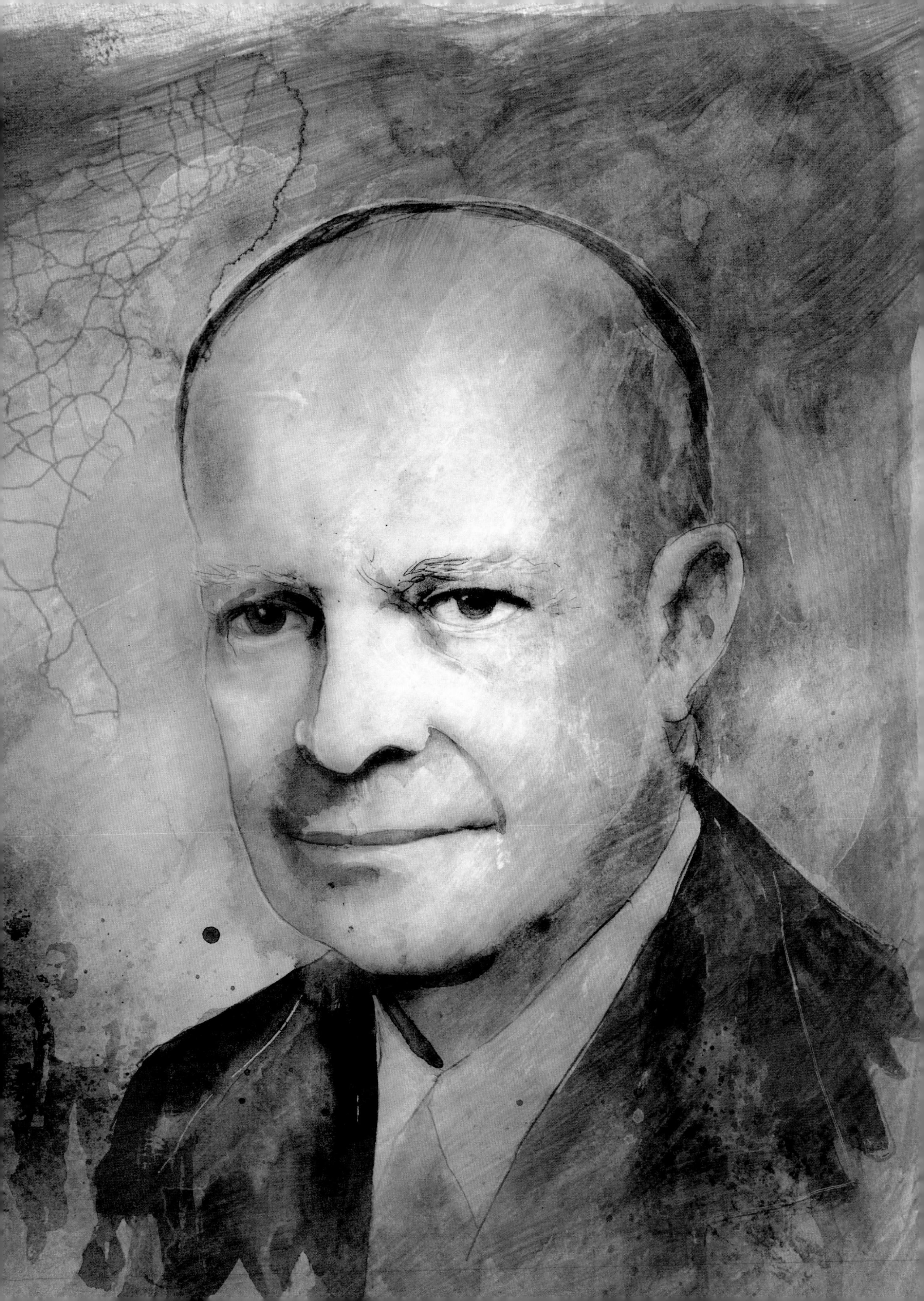

John F. Kennedy

35th President of the United States (1961-63)

Born: May 29, 1917, Brookline, Mass.
Died: Nov. 22, 1963, Dallas, Tex.
Profession: Author, Public Official
Political Affiliation: Democrat

Under a plan created by the previous Eisenhower administration, U.S.-trained Cuban insurgents were to invade Cuba and instigate an uprising among the Cuban people in hopes of removing Communist Fidel Castro from power. On April 17, 1961, Kennedy ordered the previously planned invasion of Cuba to proceed. It failed horribly and was known as the Bay of Pigs Invasion.

The Cuban Missile Crisis began on October 14, 1962, when American U-2 spy planes took photographs of a Soviet intermediate-range ballistic missile site under construction in Cuba. Kennedy faced a dilemma: if the United States attacked the sites, it might lead to nuclear war with the U.S.S.R., but if the U.S. did nothing, it would endure the threat of nuclear weapons being launched from close range. Because the weapons were in such proximity, the U.S. might have been unable to retaliate if they were launched pre-emptively. Following a tense stand-off, Kennedy and Soviet Premier Nikita Khrushche reached an agreement. Khrushchev agreed to remove the missiles subject to UN inspections if the United States publicly promised never to invade Cuba and quietly removed U.S. missiles stationed in Turkey.

Kennedy asked Congress to create the Peace Corps. Through this program, Americans volunteer to help underdeveloped nations with programs such as education, farming, health care, and construction.

He sent 16,000 military advisors and U.S. Special Forces to Vietnam to fight the Communists. Kennedy also agreed to the use of free-fire zones, napalm, defoliants, and jet planes. United States involvement in the area escalated until regular U.S. forces were directly fighting the Vietnam War in the next administration.

Kennedy signed the Partial Test Ban Treaty against nuclear weapons into law in August 1963.

In 1963, the Kennedy administration backed a coup against the government of Iraq headed by General Abdel Karim Kassem, who five years earlier had deposed the Western-allied Iraqi monarchy. The CIA helped the new Baath Party government, led by Abdul Salam Arif, in ridding the country of suspected leftists and Communists.

On June 11, 1963, President Kennedy intervened when Alabama Governor George Wallace blocked the doorway to the University of Alabama to stop two African American students from enrolling. Kennedy proposed what would become the Civil Rights Act of 1964.

Kennedy was assassinated in Dallas, on November 22, 1963, while on a political trip to Texas. Lee Harvey Oswald was arrested but denied shooting anyone, claiming he was a patsy, and was killed by Jack Ruby on November 24, before he could be indicted or tried.

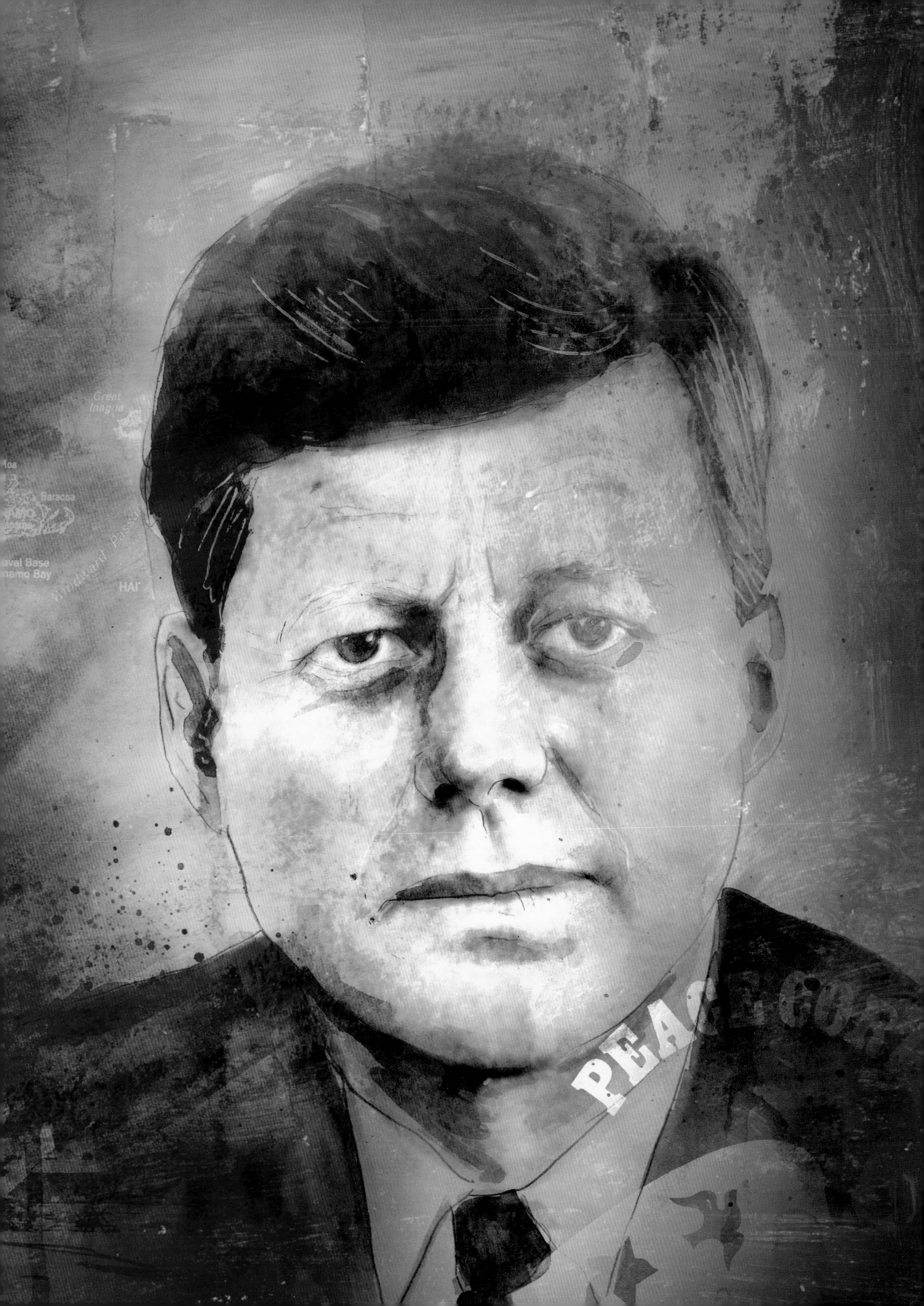
Great
Inagua
Baracoa

Lyndon B. Johnson

36th President of the United States (1963-69)

Born: Aug. 27, 1908, near Johnson City, Tex.
Died: Jan. 22, 1973, near Johnson City, Tex.
Profession: Teacher, Public Official
Political Affiliation: Democrat

Two hours and eight minutes after President Kennedy was shot two cars in front of him in a Dealey Plaza motorcade, Johnson was sworn in as President.

In conjunction with the civil rights movement, Johnson overcame southern resistance and convinced Congress to pass the Civil Rights Act of 1964, which outlawed most forms of racial segregation.

The Great Society program became Johnson's agenda for Congress in January 1965: aid to education, attack on disease, Medicare, urban renewal, beautification, conservation, development of depressed regions, a wide-scale fight against poverty, control and prevention of crime, and removal of obstacles to the right to vote.

1965 saw the Medicare amendment to the Social Security Act.

There were many riots in black ghettos. The biggest wave came in April 1968, when riots occurred in over a hundred cities in the wake of the assassination of Dr. Martin Luther King.

Johnson increasingly focused on the American military effort in Vietnam, and firmly believed in the "Domino Theory" and that his containment policy required America to make a serious effort to stop all Communist expansion.

The Gulf of Tonkin Resolution, which gave the president the exclusive right to use military force without consulting the Senate, was based on a false pretext, as he later admitted.

Johnson escalated the increasingly unpopular Vietnam War effort continuously from 1964 to 1968.

As the Democratic Party began to split apart over the war, Johnson announced he would not run for re-election in 1968.

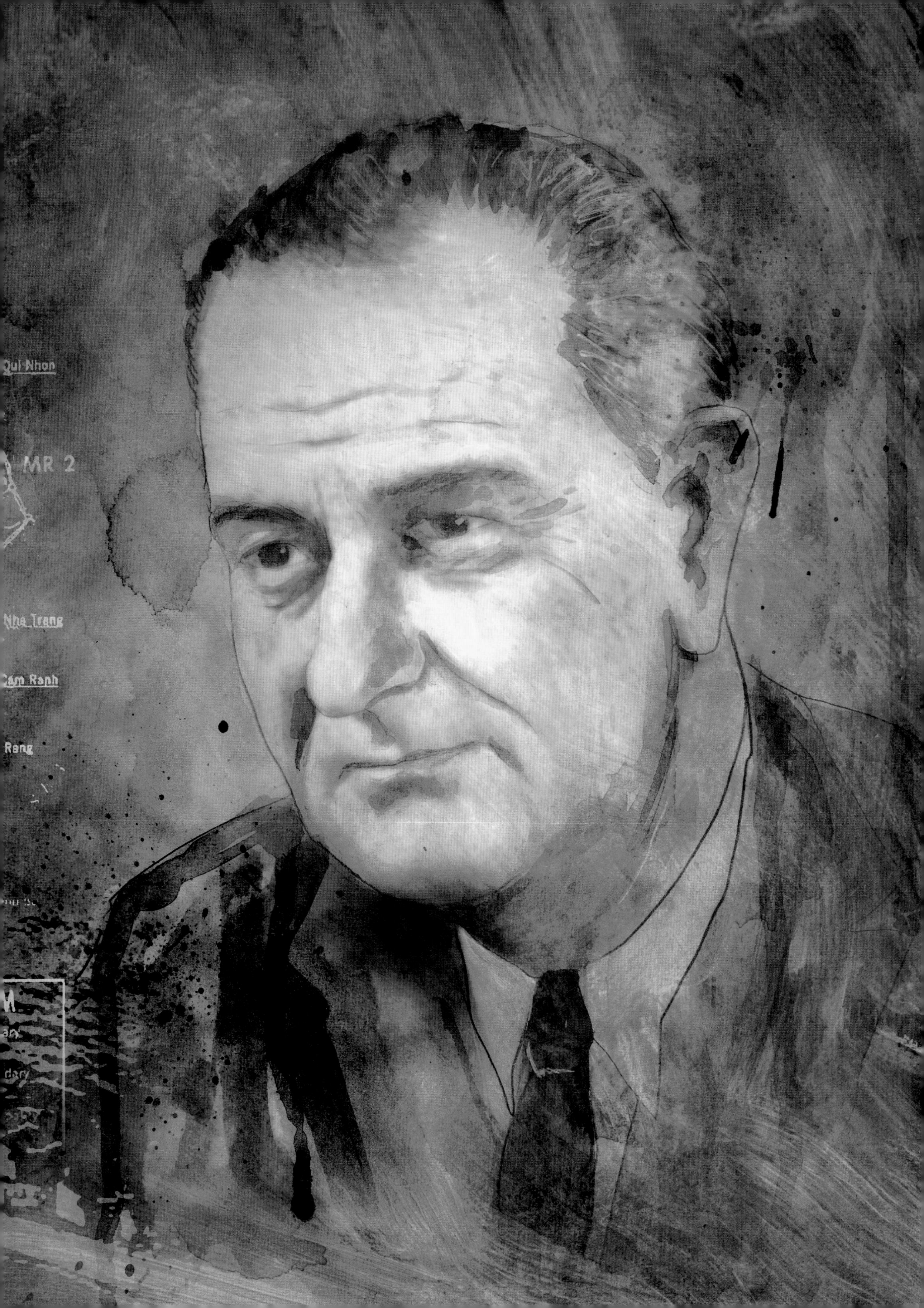
Qui Nhon
MR 2
Nha Trang
Cam Ranh
Rang

Richard M. Nixon

37th President of the United States (1969-74)

Born: Jan. 9, 1913, Yorba Linda, Calif.
Died: Apr. 22, 1994, New York City
Profession: Lawyer, Public Official
Political Affiliation: Republican

Nixon is credited with creating the modern day Imperial Presidency, in which the presidency retains a high level of control over government policy and decisions.

Nixon imposed wage and price controls, indexed Social Security for inflation, and created Supplemental Security Income.

He eradicated the last remnants of the gold standard, created the Environmental Protection Agency (EPA), the Drug Enforcement Administration (DEA), and the Occupational Safety and Health Administration (OSHA).

Under the Nixon Doctrine, a strategy of replacing American troops with Vietnamese troops also called "Vietnamization," American involvement in the war steadily declined from a troop strength of 543,000 to zero in 1973.

Nixon approved a secret bombing campaign of Cambodia in March 1969 to destroy what was believed to be the headquarters of the National Front for the Liberation of Vietnam, and later escalated the conflict by bombing Laos.

Nixon sent Secretary of State Henry Kissinger on a secret mission to China in July 1971, after which a stunned world was told that Nixon intended to visit Communist China the following year. In February 1972, President and Mrs. Nixon travelled to China, where the president was to engage in direct talks with Mao Zedong. This visit ushered in a new era of Chinese-American relations.

He engaged in intense negotiations with his Soviet counterpart, and out of this "summit meeting" came agreements for increased trade and two landmark arms control treaties: SALT I, the first comprehensive limitation pact signed by the two superpowers, and the Anti-Ballistic Missile Treaty, which banned the development of systems designed to intercept incoming missiles.

In 1972, Nixon was re-elected in one of the biggest landslide election victories in U.S. political history, defeating Senator George McGovern and garnering over 60% of the popular vote.

Nixon strongly supported Israel in the 1967 Yom Kippur War but the victory for its ally, and the support provided to them by the United States, came at the cost of the 1973 oil crisis as the members of OPEC decided to raise oil prices in response to the American support of Israel.

The Watergate Scandal covered an array of illegal and secret activities undertaken by Nixon or his aides during his administration. These activities did not come to light until several men were caught breaking into Democratic Party headquarters at the Watergate Hotel in Washington, D.C., on June 17, 1972. Despite Nixon's best efforts a secret recording, known as the Smoking Gun Tape, was released on August 5, 1974, and revealed that he was involved in the scandal. During the Watergate scandal, Nixon's approval rating fell to 23%. He resigned the office of the presidency on August 9, 1974.

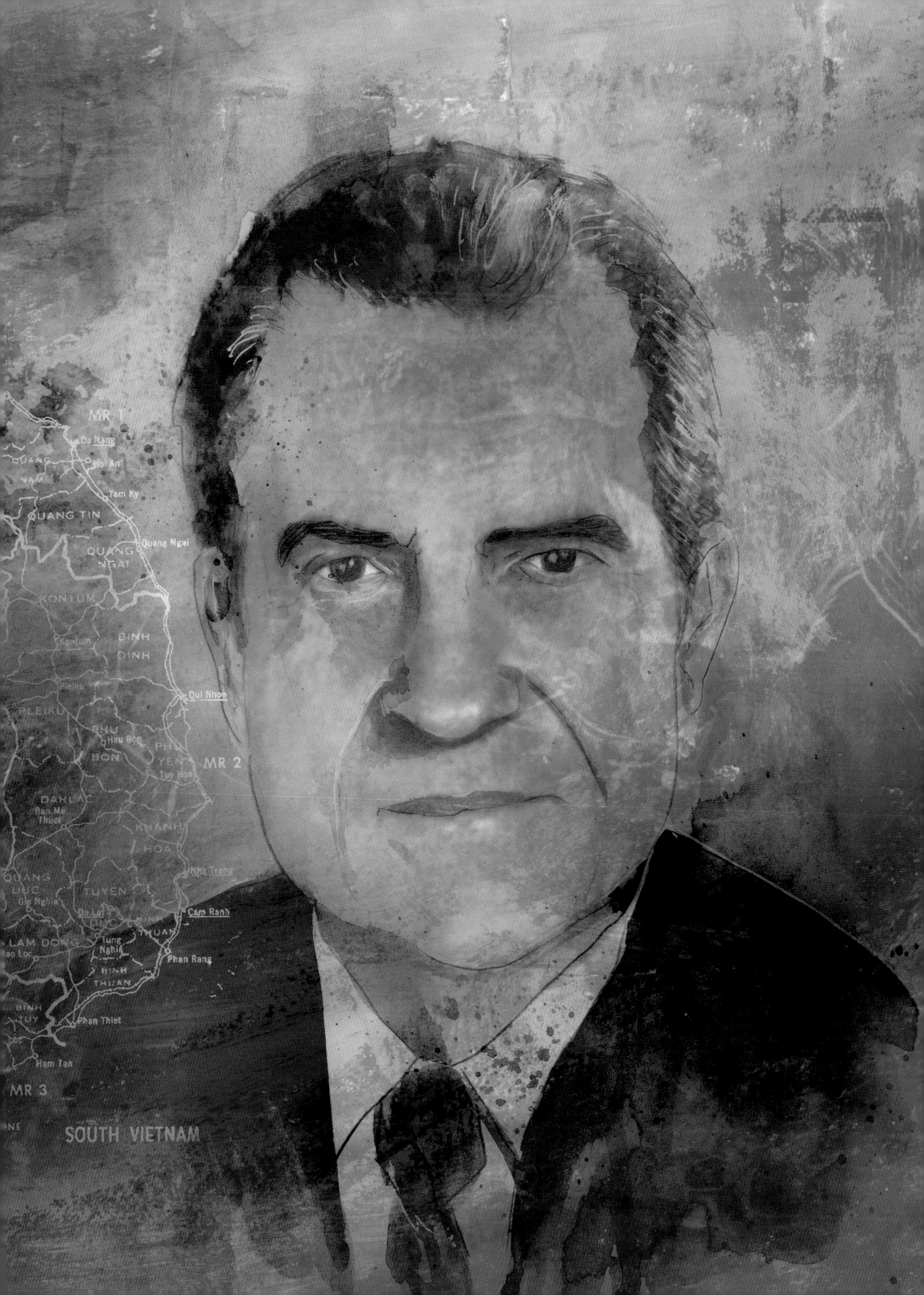

MR 1
Da Nang
QUANG
Hoi An
NAM
Tam Ky
QUANG TIN
Quang Ngai
QUANG
NGAI
KONTUM
Kontum
BINH
DINH
Pleiku
Qui Nhon
PLEIKU
PHU
Hau Bon
BON
PHU
YEN
MR 2
Tuy Hoa
DARLAC
Ban Me
Thuot
KHANH
HOA
Nha Trang
QUANG
DUC
Gia Nghia
TUYEN
Da Lat
DUC
Cam Ranh
NINH
THUAN
LAM DONG
Tung
Nghia
Phan Rang
BINH
THUAN
BINH
TUY
Phan Thiet
Ham Tan
MR 3
SOUTH VIETNAM

Gerald Ford

38th President of the United States (1974–77)

Born: July 14, 1913, Omaha, Nebr.
Died: December 26, Rancho Mirage, Ca.
Profession: Lawyer, Public Official
Political Affiliation: Republican

On September 8, 1974, in a highly controversial move, Ford gave Nixon a full and unconditional pardon for any crimes he may have committed against the United States while president. Historians believe the controversy was one of the major reasons Ford lost the election in 1976.

All American military forces had withdrawn from Vietnam in 1973. As the North Vietnamese invaded and conquered the South in 1975, Ford ordered the final withdrawal of American civilians from Vietnam in "Operation Frequent Wind," leading to the subsequent fall of Saigon.

Ford attended the inaugural meeting of the Group of Seven (G7) industrialized nations (initially the G5) in 1975 and secured membership for Canada.

The ongoing Cyprus dispute turned into a crisis with the Turkish invasion of Cyprus, causing extreme strain within the NATO alliance. In mid-August, the government withdrew Greece from the NATO military structure; in mid-September 1974 the United States stopped military aid to Turkey.

Ford faced two assassination attempts during his presidency, occurring within three weeks of each other. While in Sacramento, California on September 5, 1975, Lynette "Squeaky" Fromme, a follower of Charles Manson, pointed a Colt 45-caliber handgun at Ford but was stopped by a Secret Service agent. Seventeen days later, another woman, Sara Jane Moore, also tried to kill Ford while he was visiting San Francisco, but her attempt was thwarted when former marine Oliver Sipple deflected her shot.

Ford reluctantly agreed to run for office in 1976 and lost by a slim margin to Jimmy Carter.

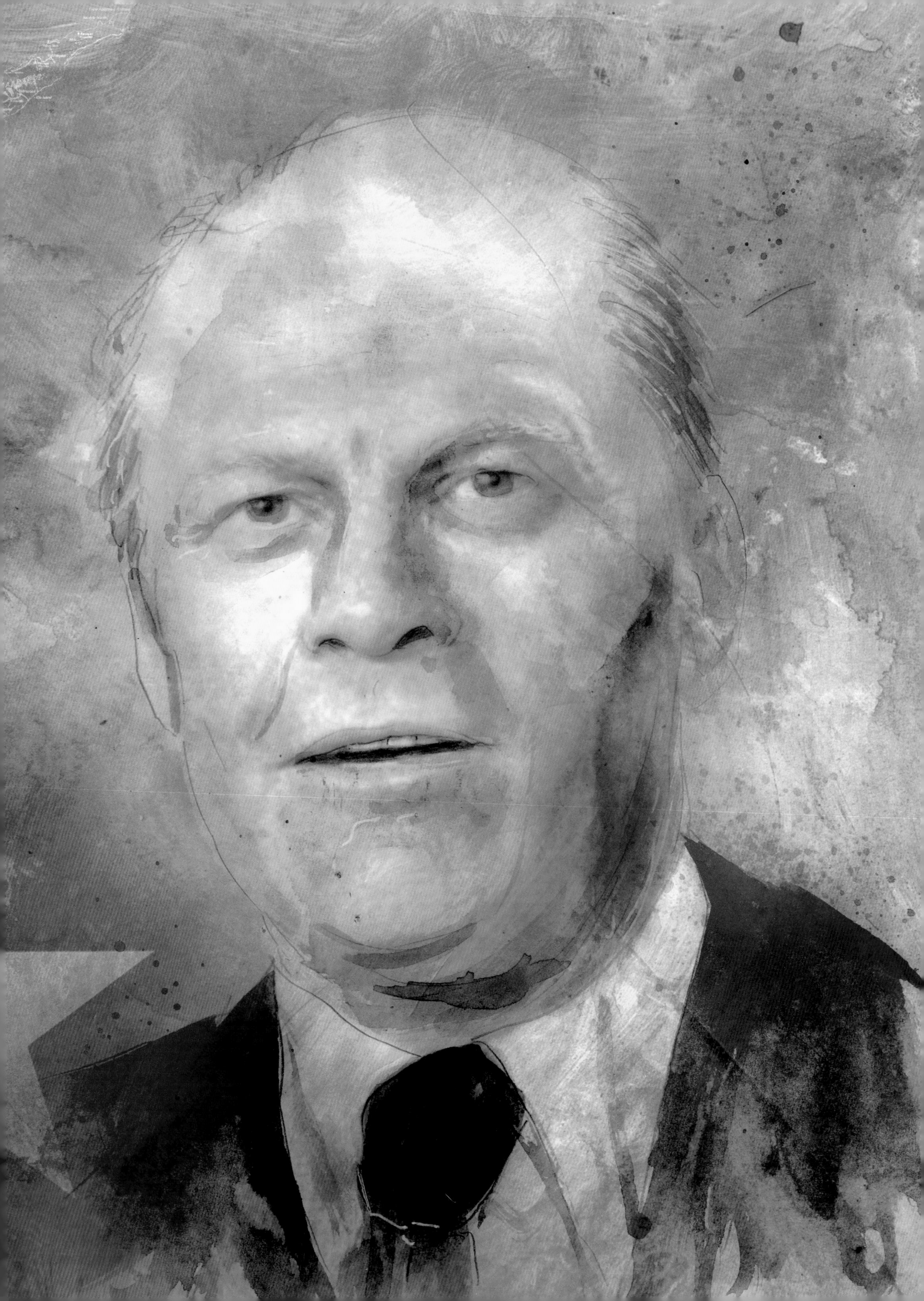

Jimmy Carter

39th President of the United States (1977-81)

Born: Oct. 1, 1924, Plains, Ga.
Profession: Farmer, Public Official
Political Affiliation: Democrat

On Carter's first day in office, January 20, 1977, he fulfilled a campaign promise by issuing an Executive Order declaring unconditional amnesty for Vietnam War-era draft evaders.

Carter's first steps in the White House were to reduce the size of the staff by one-third and order cabinet members to drive their own cars.

In 1977, Carter convinced the Democratic Congress to create the United States Department of Energy (DoE) in order to conserve energy.

During Carter's administration, the economy suffered double-digit inflation, coupled with very high interest rates, oil shortages, high unemployment, and slow economic growth.

The U.S. prime interest rate hit 21.5% in December 1980, the highest rate in U.S. history under any President.

Carter cut the defense budget by $6 billion. One of his first acts was to order the unilateral removal of all nuclear weapons from South Korea and announce his intention to cut back the number of U.S. troops stationed there.

Carter negotiated the1978 Camp David Accords, a peace agreement between Israel and Egypt.

One of the most controversial moves of President Carter's presidency was the final negotiation and signature of the Panama Canal Treaties in September 1977. Those treaties, which essentially would transfer control of the American-built Panama Canal to the nation of Panama, were bitterly opposed by a majority of the American public and by the Republican Party.

When the Iranian Revolution broke out in Iran and the Shah was overthrown, the United States did not intervene directly. The Shah went into permanent exile. Carter initially refused him entry to the United States, but eventually relented. In response to the Shah's entry into the U.S., Iranian militants seized the American embassy in Tehran, taking 52 Americans hostage. The hostage crisis continued and dominated the last year of Carter's presidency. The subsequent responses to the crisis, including the unsuccessful attempt to rescue the hostages by military means, were largely seen as contributing to Carter's defeat in the 1980 election.

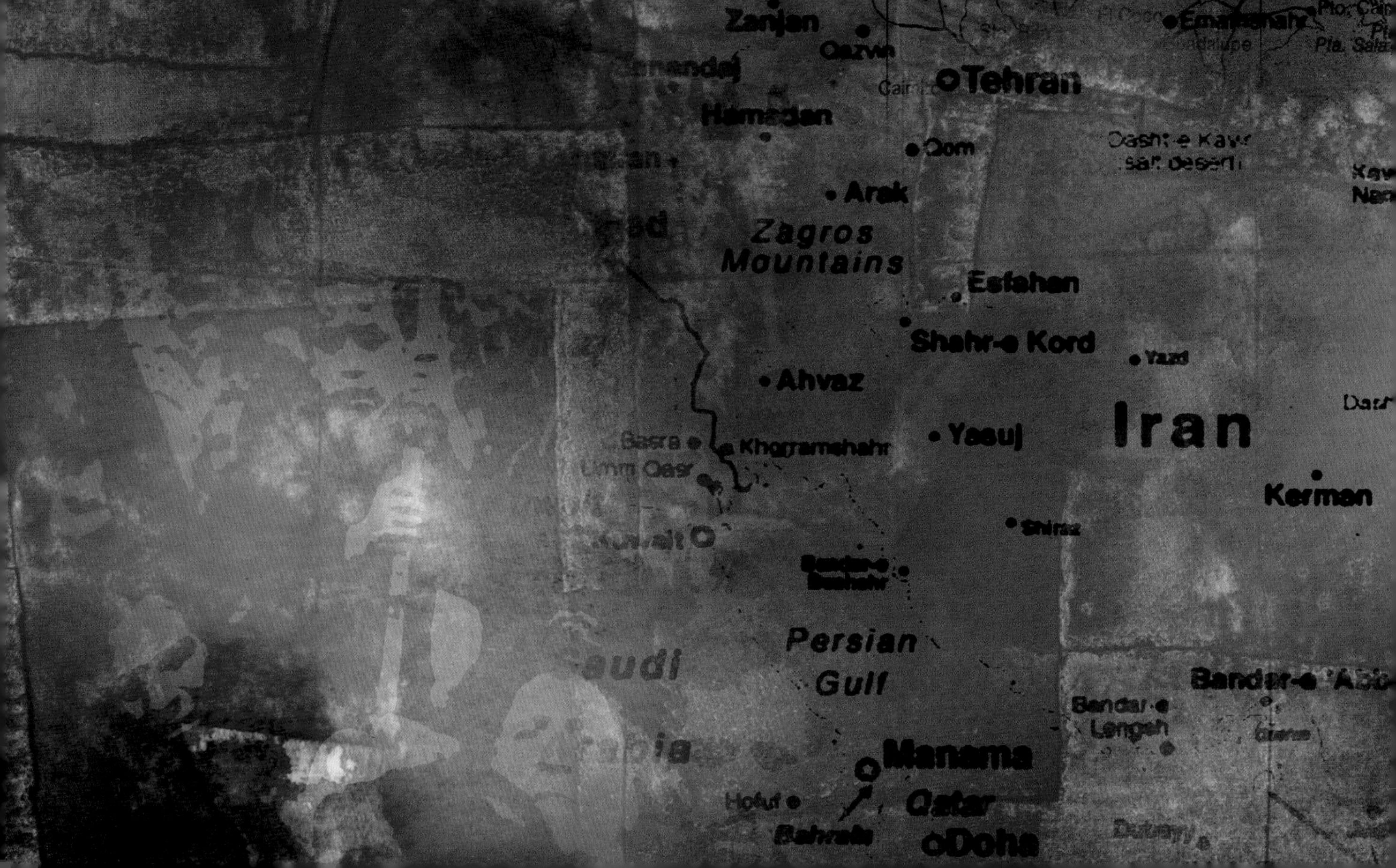
Zanjan
Qazvin
Tehran
Hamadan
Qom
Arak
Zagros Mountains
Esfahan
Shahr-e Kord
Ahvaz
Yasuj
Iran
Kerman
Basra
Khorramshahr
Persian Gulf
Manama
Qatar
Doha

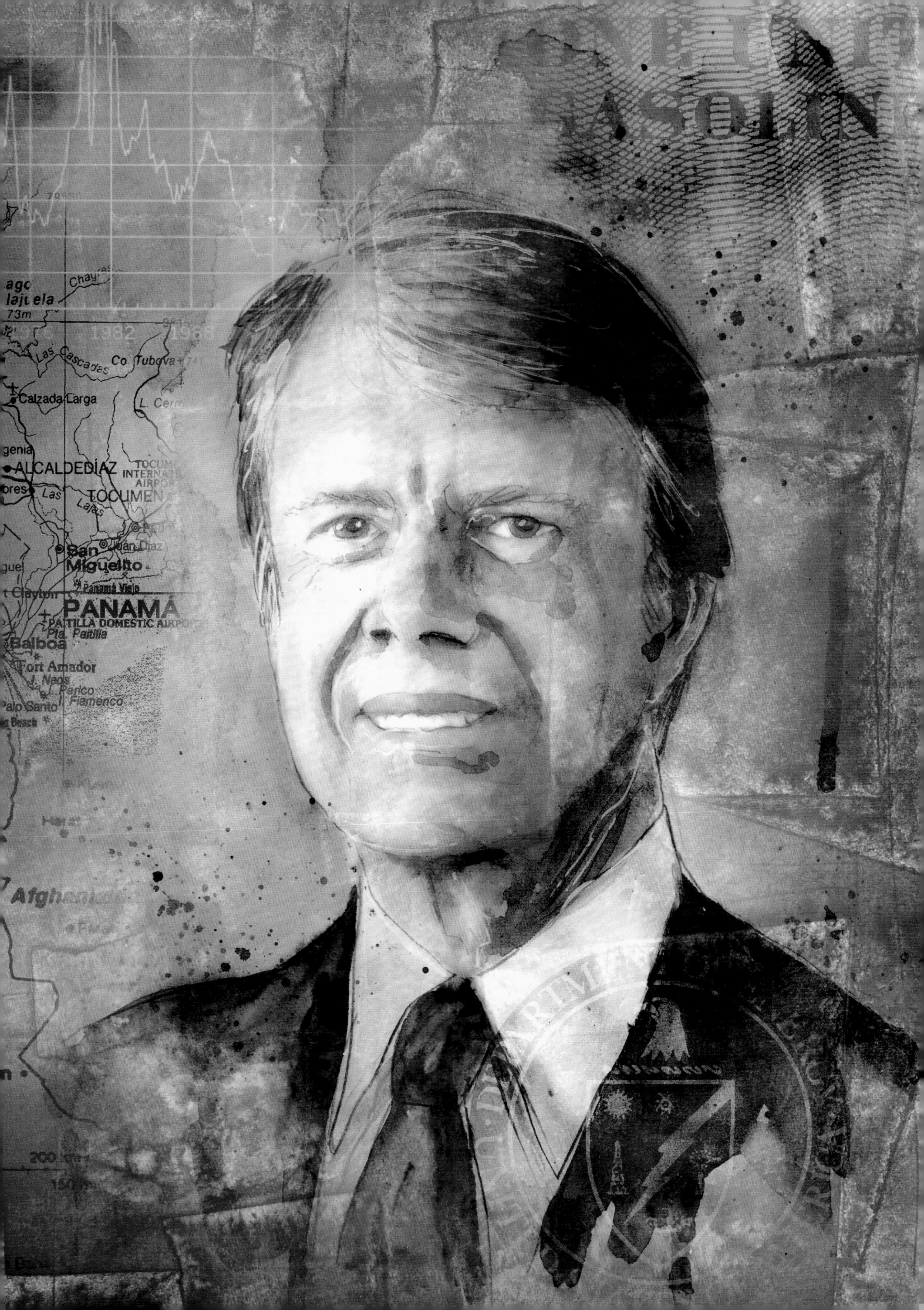

1982
Las Cascadas
Calzada Larga
ALCALDEDÍAZ
TOCUMEN
San Miguelito
Panamá Viejo
PANAMÁ
Pta. Paitilla
Balboa
Fort Amador
I. Naos
I. Perico
Flamenco
Palo Santo

Ronald Reagan

40th President of the United States (1981-89)
Born: Feb. 6, 1911, Tampico, Ill.
Died: June 5, 2004, Bel Air, Calif.
Profession: Actor, Public Official
Political Affiliation: Republican

To date, Reagan is the oldest man elected to the office of the presidency.

Reagan appointed the first female Supreme Court Justice, Sandra Day O'Connor.

The Reagan presidency began in a dramatic manner: as Reagan was giving his inaugural address, 52 U.S. hostages held by Iran for 444 days were set free.

On March 30, 1981, Reagan, along with his press secretary James Brady and two others, were shot by a would-be assassin, John Hinckley, Jr. He survived the attempt, the bullet missing his heart by less than one inch. Hinckley was found not guilty by reason of insanity.

Reagan implemented policies based on supply-side economics and advocated a laissez-faire philosophy, which would become known as "Reaganomics." He promoted tax cuts as potentially stimulating the economy enough to expand the tax base, offsetting the revenue loss due to reduced rates of taxation, a theory that entered political discussion as the Laffer curve.

As part of a peacekeeping force in Beirut during the Lebanese Civil War, American troops who had been earlier deployed by Reagan were attacked on October 23, 1983. The barracks bombing resulted in the deaths of 241 Americans by suicide bombers.

Reagan escalated the Cold War, accelerating a reversal from the policy of détente, which began in 1979 following the Soviet invasion of Afghanistan. Reagan ordered a massive build-up of the U.S. military.

In the 1984 election against Democrat Walter Mondale, Reagan won a record 525 electoral votes.

The Reagan administration was criticized for its slow response to the growing HIV-AIDS epidemic.

The Space Shuttle Challenger disintegrated soon after launch on January 28, 1986.

Tensions rose with Libya in early April 1986, when a bomb exploded in a Berlin nightclub resulting in the injuries of 63 American military personnel and one death. Citing "irrefutable proof" that Libya had directed the terrorist bombing, Reagan authorized the use of force against the country. In the late evening of April 15, 1986, the United States launched a series of air strikes on ground targets in Libya.

In 1986, Reagan signed the Immigration Reform and Control Act (IRCA). The act made it illegal to knowingly hire or recruit illegal immigrants, required employers to attest to their employees' immigration status, and granted amnesty to approximately three million illegal immigrants.

The Iran-Contra affair stemmed from the use of proceeds from covert arms sales to Iran to fund the Contras in Nicaragua, which had been specifically outlawed by an act of Congress. It became the largest political scandal in the United States during the 1980s. Reagan professed ignorance of the plot's existence.

The Berlin Wall was torn down starting in 1989, thanks in large part to Reagan's efforts.

On July 13, 1985, Reagan underwent surgery at Bethesda Naval Hospital to remove cancerous polyps from his colon. This caused the first-ever invocation of the acting president clause of the 25th Amendment. The surgery lasted just under three hours and was successful.

BRILLIANT
EYES

BOOST
CLE
IVI

BOOST
PHASE

VALUED
DEFENSES

US debt

42,000

Billions of US dollars

6,000

4,000

2,000

0

1929 1933   41 845 849 859 957 961 969 1973

George Bush

41st President of the United States (1989–93)

Born: June 12, 1924, Milton, Mass.
Profession: Businessman, Public Official
Political Affiliation: Republican

The Soviet Union collapsed early in his presidency.

Deficits spawned by the Reagan years had ballooned to $220 billion in 1990, three times its size in 1980. Bush was dedicated to curbing the deficit, believing that America could not continue to be a leader in the world without doing so.

Bush signed the Americans with Disabilities Act of 1990, one of the most pro-civil rights bills in decades.

"Operation Just Cause" was a large-scale American military operation to invade Panama and remove Panamanian leader Manuel Noriega, a once U.S.-supportive leader who was later accused of spying for Fidel Castro and using Panama to traffic drugs into the United States. It was the first conflict in more than 40 years that was not Cold War related.

On August 1, 1990, Iraq, led by Saddam Hussein, invaded its oil-rich neighbor to the south, Kuwait. Bush condemned the invasion and began rallying opposition to Iraq with U.S., European, Asian, and Middle Eastern allies.

In what became known as the Persian Gulf War, early on the morning of January 17, 1991, allied forces attacked Iraq and Iraqi-occupied Kuwait. Allied forces penetrated Iraqi lines and pushed toward Kuwait City, while on the west side of the country forces were intercepting the retreating Iraqi army. Bush made the decision to stop the offensive after a mere 100 hours, saying that he wanted to minimize U.S. casualties, having liberated Kuwait. Bush's approval ratings skyrocketed after the successful offensive.

In July 1991, the Strategic Arms Reduction Treaty (START I) was signed by Bush and Soviet leader Mikhail Gorbachev in Moscow.

After the dissolution of the U.S.S.R. in 1991, President Bush and Gorbachev declared a U.S.-Russian strategic partnership, marking the end of the Cold War.

Bush's administration, along with the Progressive Conservative Canadian Prime Minister Brian Mulroney, spearheaded the negotiations of the North American Free Trade Agreement (NAFTA), which would eliminate the majority of tariffs on products traded among the United States, Canada, and Mexico, to encourage trade amongst the countries.

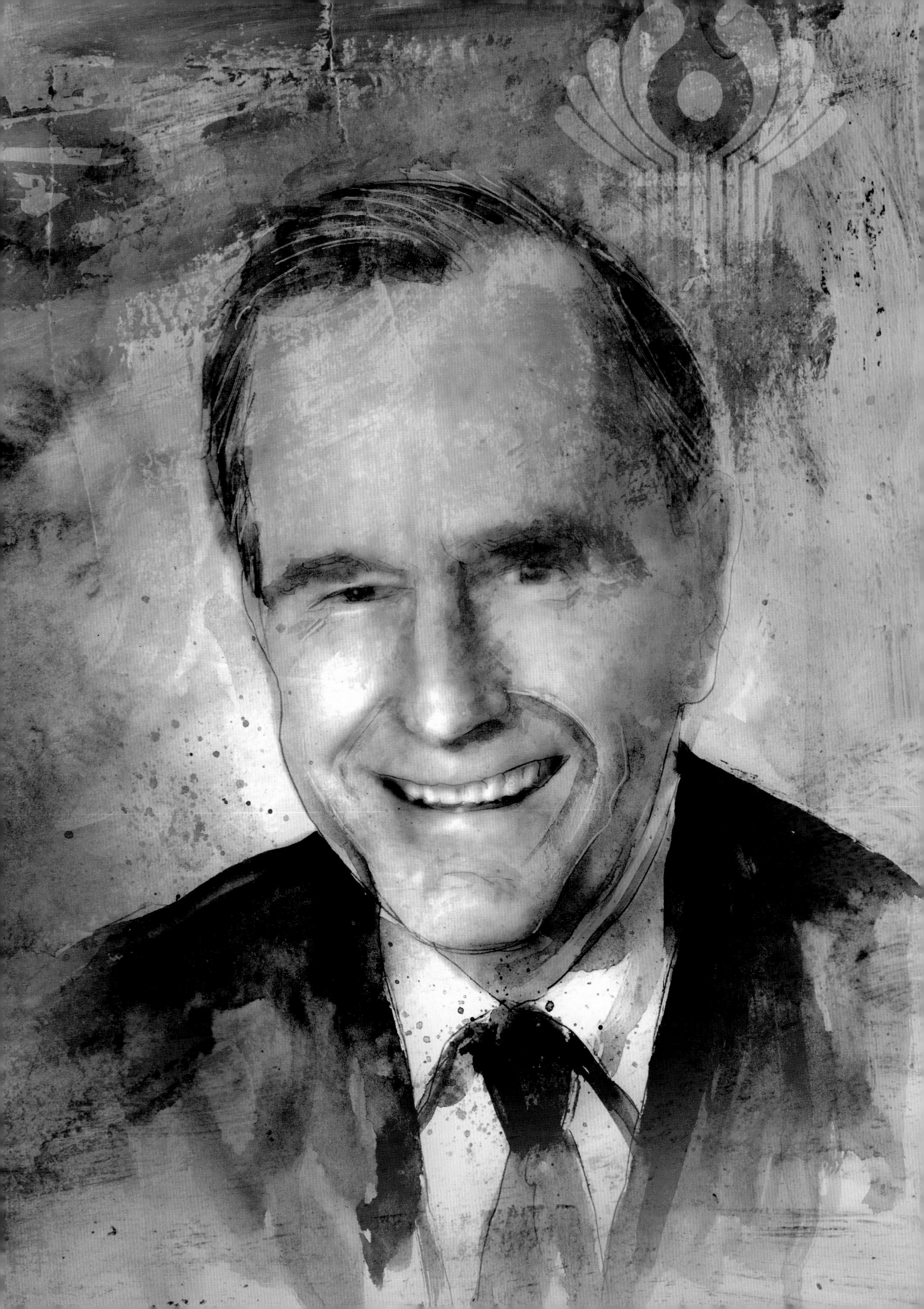

Bill Clinton

42nd President of the United States (1993-2001)

Born: Aug. 19, 1946, Hope, Ark.
Profession: Lawyer, Public Official
Political Affiliation: Democrat

Shortly after taking office, Clinton signed the Family and Medical Leave Act of 1993, which required large employers to allow employees to take unpaid leave for pregnancy or a serious medical condition.

Clinton's attempt to fulfill another campaign promise of allowing openly homosexual men and women to serve in the armed forces garnered criticism from the left and from the right. After much debate, Congress implemented the "Don't ask, don't tell" policy.

In 1993, Clinton controversially supported ratification of the North American Free Trade Agreement by the U.S. Senate.

The Battle of Mogadishu occurred in Somalia in 1993. During the operation, two U.S. MH-60 Black Hawk helicopters were shot down by rocket-propelled grenade attacks. Eighteen American soldiers were killed and 73 others were wounded with one taken prisoner. Some of the American bodies were dragged through the streets and broadcast on television news programs. In response, U.S. forces were withdrawn from Somalia and later conflicts were approached with fewer soldiers on the ground.

Frank Eugene Corder crashed a stolen Cessna 150 onto the South Lawn of the White House early on September 12, 1994, apparently trying to hit the building; he was the sole casualty.

The Clinton administration launched the first official White House website on October 21, 1994.

In the 1996 presidential election, Clinton was re-elected, becoming the first Democrat to win presidential re-election since Franklin Roosevelt.

Clinton's sexual relationship with a 22-year-old White House intern named Monica Lewinsky resulted in the Lewinsky scandal. The Republican-controlled House voted to impeach Clinton in 1998, making him the second United States president to be impeached after Andrew Johnson.

Clinton enacted the Digital Millennium Copyright Act on October 21, 1998. It served as the first significant amendment to the Copyright Act since 1976.

To stop the ethnic cleansing and genocide of Albanians by nationalist Serbians in the former Federal Republic of Yugoslavia's province of Kosovo, Clinton authorized the use of American troops in a NATO bombing campaign against Yugoslavia in 1999.

In November, 2000, Clinton became the first president to visit Vietnam since the end of the Vietnam War.

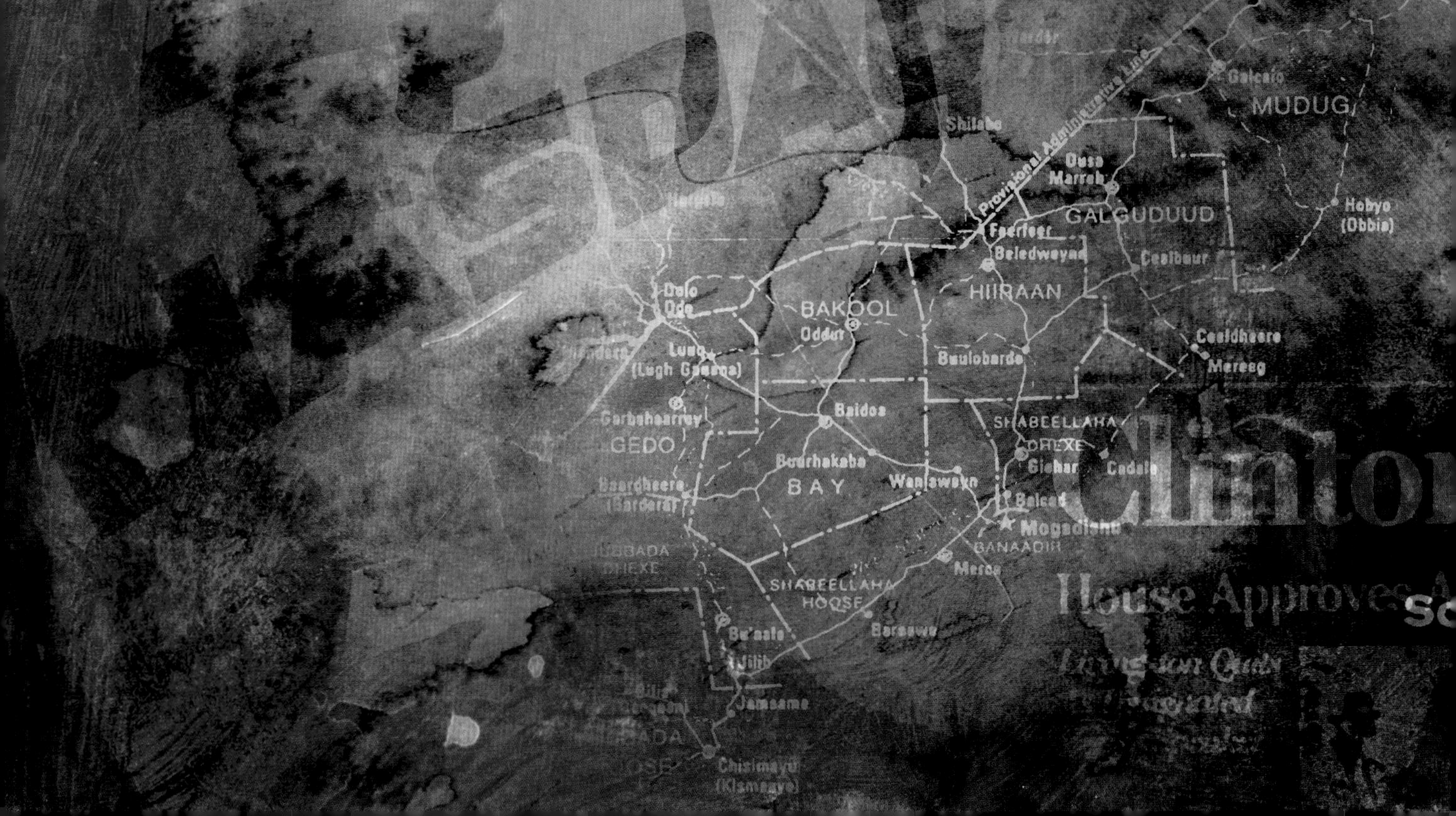

MUDUG
GALGUDUUD
HIIRAAN
BAKOOL
GEDO
BAY
Baidoa
Mogadishu
Clinton
House Approves

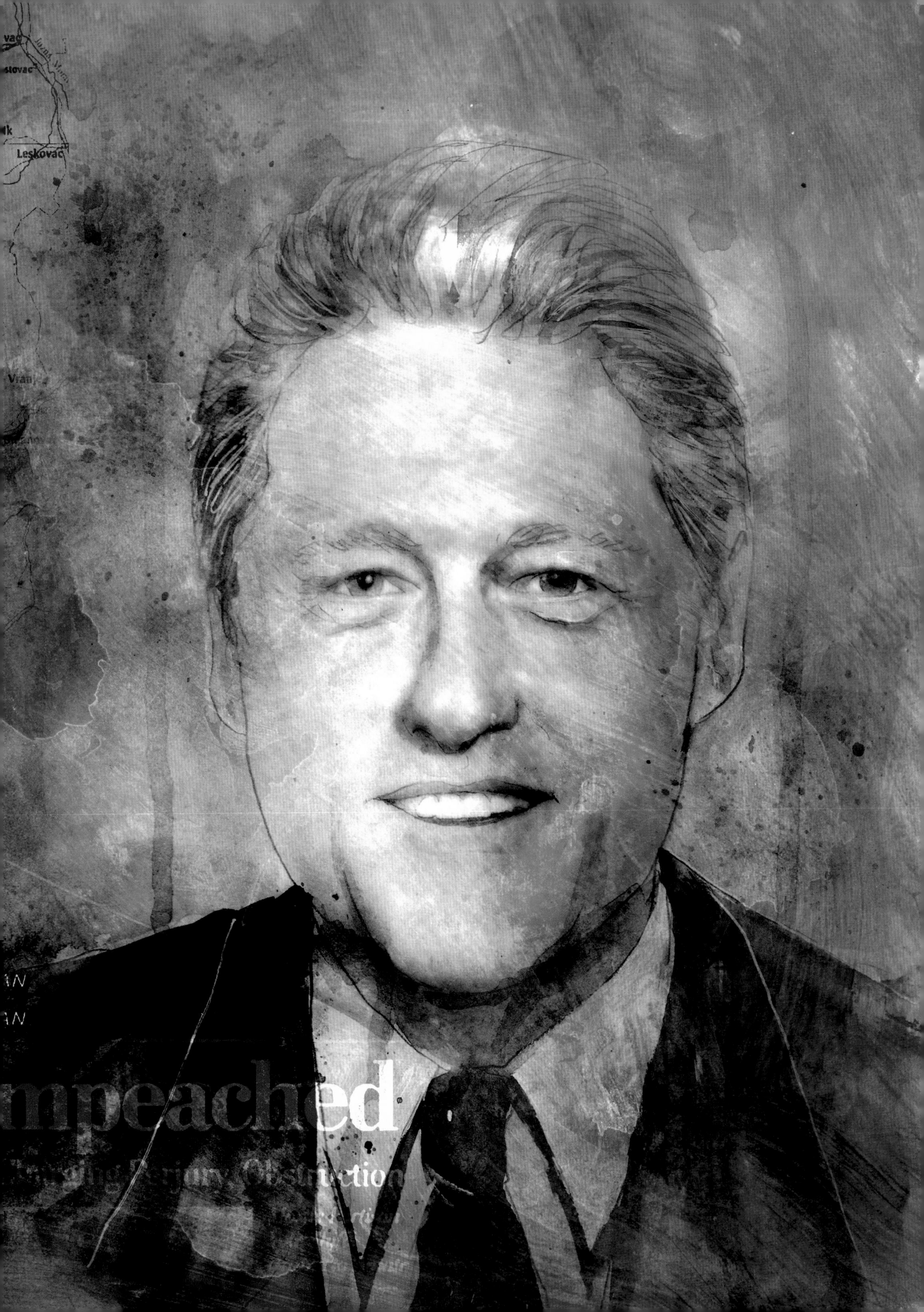
Leskovac
Vranje
mpeached

George W. Bush

43rd President of the United States (2001-2009)

Born: July 6, 1946, New Haven, Conn.
Profession: Business Executive, Public Official
Political Affiliation: Republican

In the 2000 election, Bush lost the popular vote by 543,895 votes, surpassing the previous record set in 1876. This made him one of three presidents elected without receiving a plurality of the popular vote. The closeness of the Florida outcome where Bush eventually received enough electoral votes to win, led to a recount. Two initial counts went to Bush, but the outcome was tied up in courts for a month until reaching the U.S. Supreme Court. On December 9, in the Bush v. Gore case, the machine recount in Florida stated that Bush had won the Florida vote by a margin of 537 votes out of six million cast.

Under the Bush Administration, real GDP has grown at an average annual rate of 2.5 percent, considerably below the average for business cycles from 1949 to 2000.

On September 11, 2001, terrorists hijacked passenger aircraft and flew them into the World Trade Center, killing roughly three thousand people. In response, Bush launched the War on Terror, in which the U.S. military and an international coalition invaded Afghanistan in order to remove the extremist Islamic Taliban regime.

The Bush Administration proceeded to assert a right and intention to engage in pre-emptive war, also called preventive war, in response to perceived threats. This in part became known as the Bush Doctrine.

The Iraq War, also known as the Second Gulf War or the Occupation of Iraq, is an ongoing military campaign which began on March 20, 2003 with the invasion of Iraq by a multinational force led by and composed largely of U.S. and United Kingdom troops with the goal of removing President Saddam Hussein. The Bush Administration charged that Iraq was seeking to develop and use weapons of mass destruction.

The U.S.-led coalition occupied Iraq and attempted to establish a new democratic government; however, violence against coalition forces and among various sectarian groups soon led to asymmetric warfare with an Iraqi insurgency.

On November 27, 2008, a new Iraqi Parliament ratified a Status of Forces Agreement with the United States, establishing that Coalition combat forces will withdraw from Iraqi cities by June 30, 2009, and will be completely out of Iraq by December 31, 2011.

Bush issued an executive order authorizing the NSA to monitor communications between suspected terrorists outside the U.S. and parties within the U.S. without obtaining a warrant pursuant to the Foreign Intelligence Surveillance Act, maintaining that the warrant requirements of FISA were implicitly superseded by the subsequent passage of the Authorization for Use of Military Force.

On May 10, 2005, Vladimir Arutyunian threw a live hand grenade toward a podium where Bush was speaking at Freedom Square in Tbilisi, Georgia.

Bush withdrew U.S. support for the Anti-Ballistic Missile Treaty (ABM) with Russia.

In 2003-2004, he authorized U.S. military intervention in Haiti and Liberia to protect U.S. interests.

On March 8, 2008, Bush vetoed H.R. 2082, a bill that would have expanded Congressional oversight over the intelligence community and banned the use of waterboarding, as well as other forms of enhanced interrogation techniques.

Hurricane Katrina, which was one of the worst natural disasters in U.S. history, struck early in Bush's second term. Katrina formed in late August during the 2005 Atlantic hurricane season and devastated much of the north-central Gulf Coast of the United States, particularly New Orleans.

Controversy arose over the Justice Department's midterm dismissal of seven U.S. Attorneys. The White House maintained the U.S. attorneys were fired for poor performance. Attorney General Alberto Gonzales would later resign over the issue.

2008 saw a shaky economy, consisting of a housing market correction, a subprime mortgage crisis, soaring oil prices, and a declining dollar value. In September, the crisis worsened and the majority of the American banking industry was consolidated into three companies.

George W. Bush

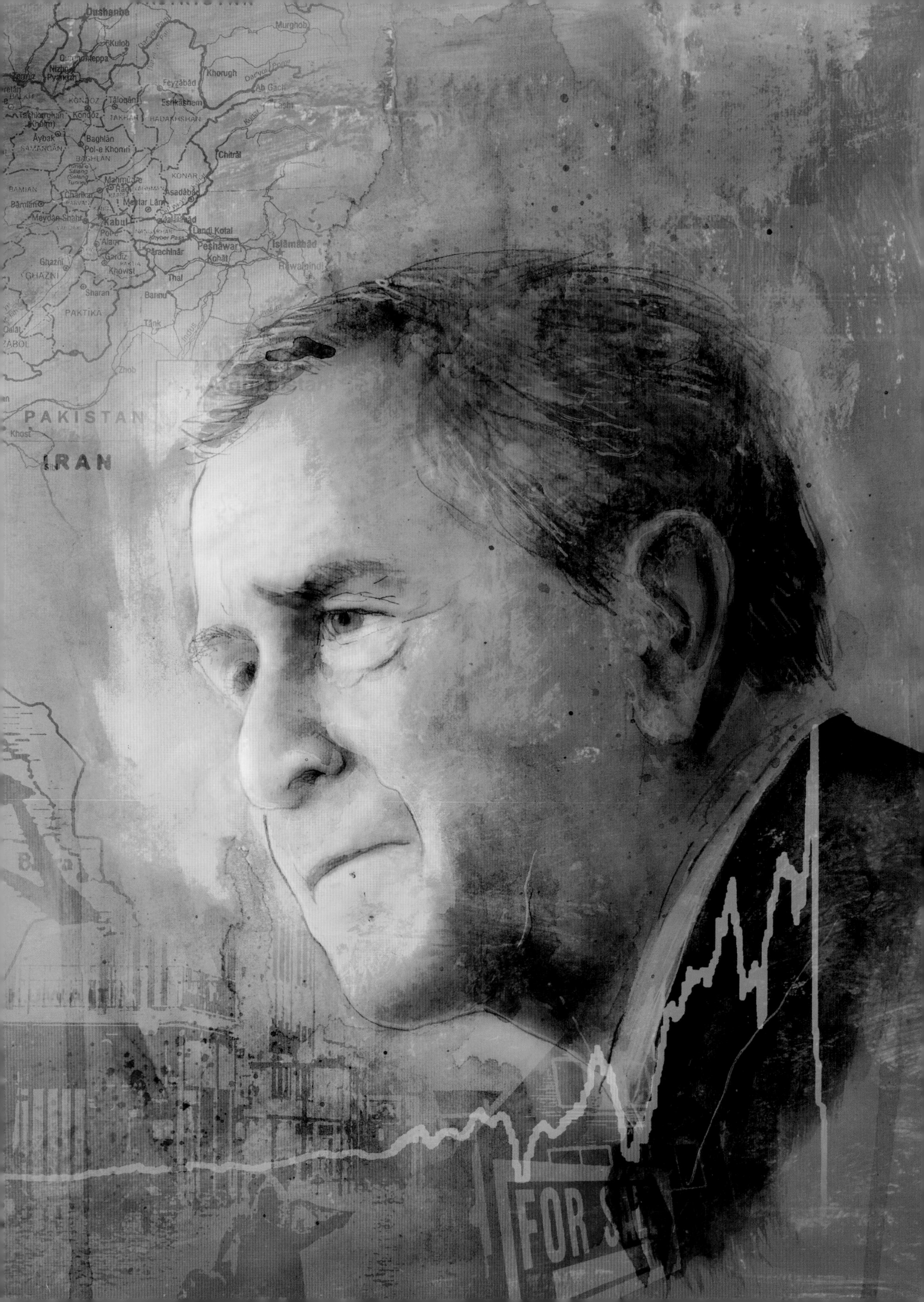
Dushanbe
Murghob
Kulob
Khorugh
Feyzābād
Eshkāshem
BADAKHSHAN
Baghlān
Pol-e Khomri
Āybak
SAMANGĀN
Chitrāl
KONAR
Asadābād
Meydān Shahr
Kabul
Jalālābād
Landi Kotal
Peshāwar
Islāmābād
Kohāt
Pārachinār
Khowst
Ghazni
GHAZNI
Thal
Bannu
Sharan
PAKTIKĀ
Tānk
Zhob
PAKISTAN
Khost
IRAN

Barack Obama

44th President of the United States (president-elect at time of printing)

Born: August 4, 1961, Honolulu, Hawaii
Profession: Lawyer, Public Official
Political Affiliation: Democrat

As president-elect at the time of printing, Obama became the first African-American to be elected to the office of President.

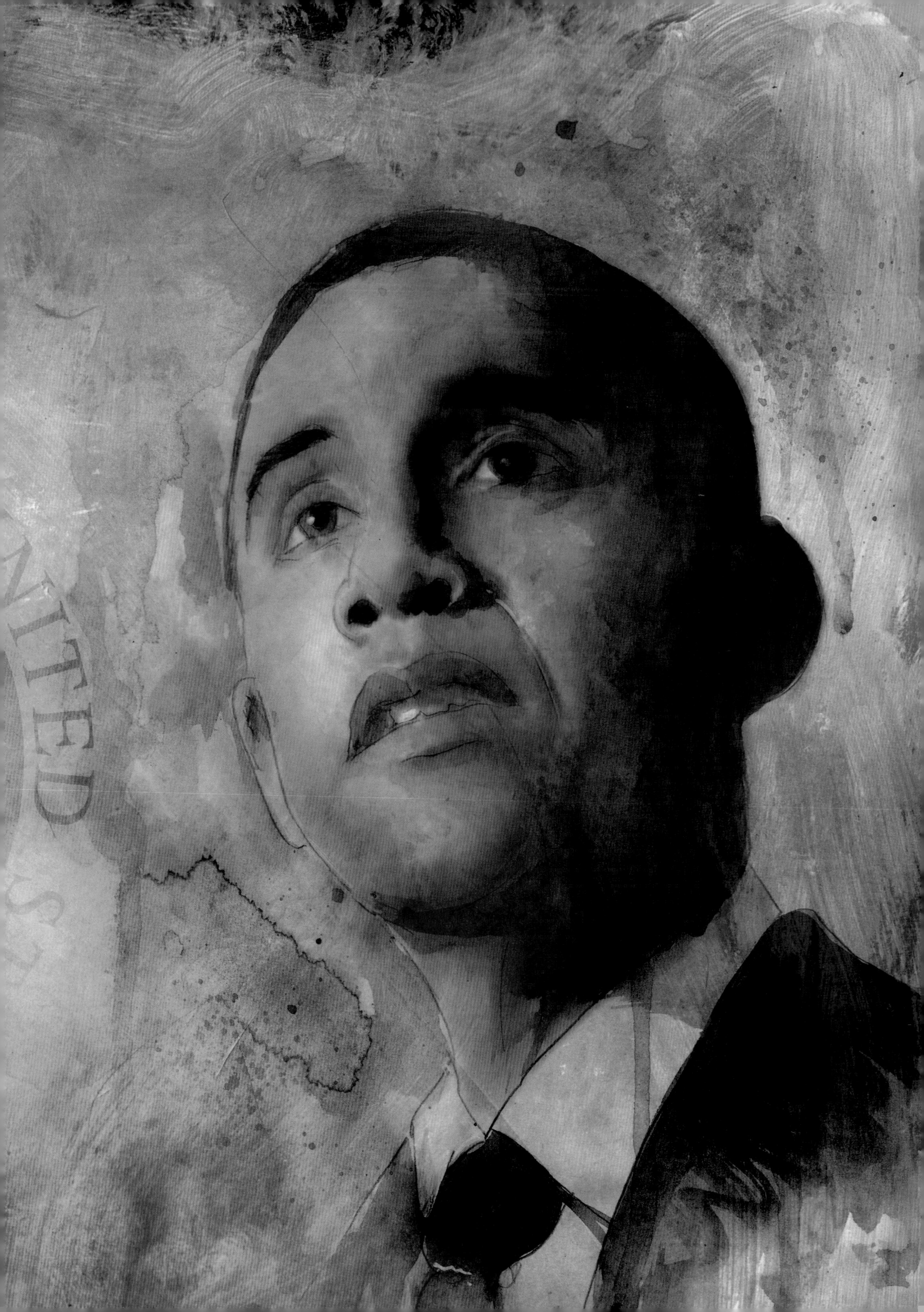
NITED

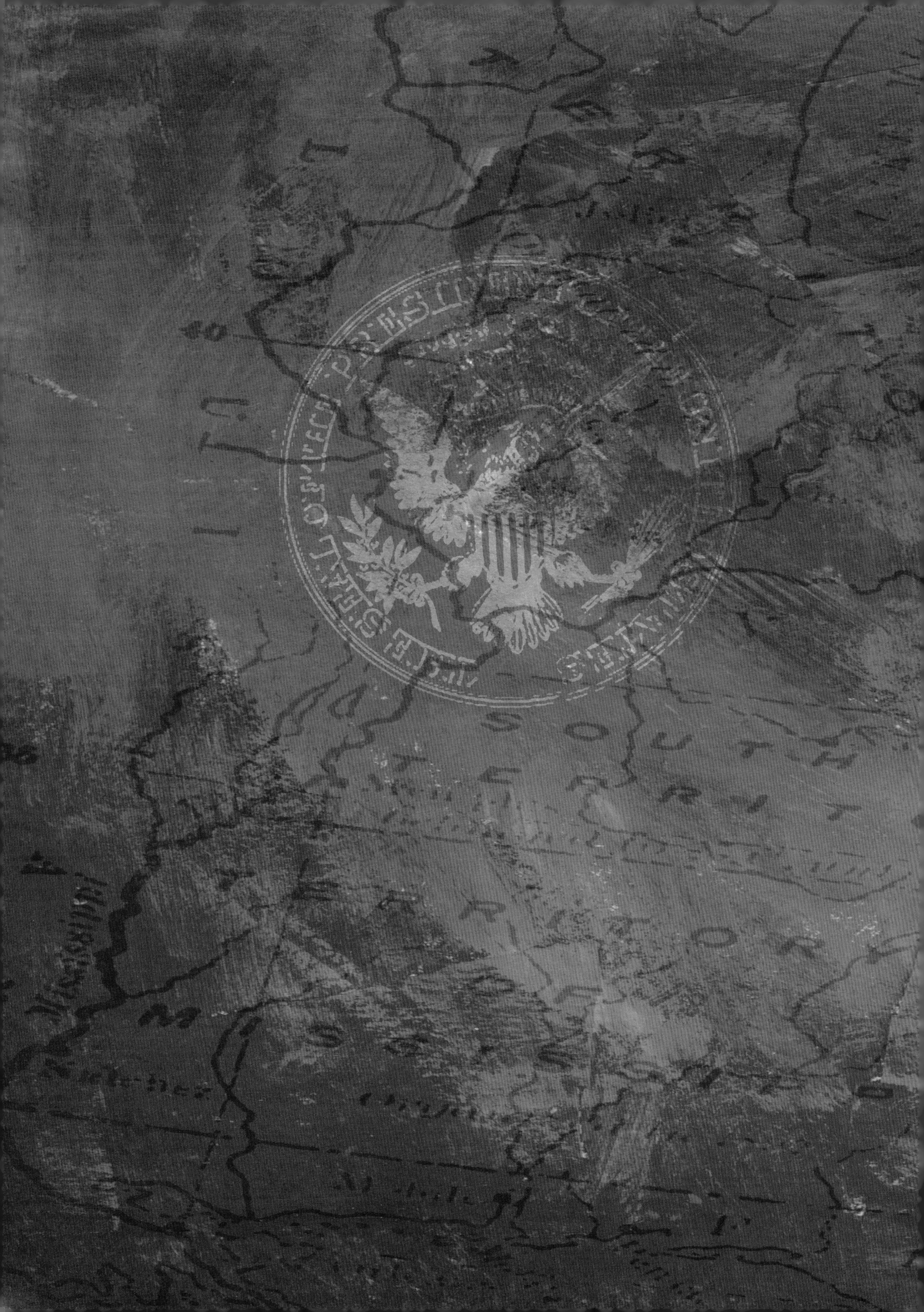

THE PRESIDENTS
OF THE
UNITED STATES
BEN TEMPLESMITH

"To announce that there must be no criticism of the president, or that we are to stand by the president, right or wrong, is not only unpatriotic and servile, but is morally treasonable to the American public."

-Theodore Roosevelt

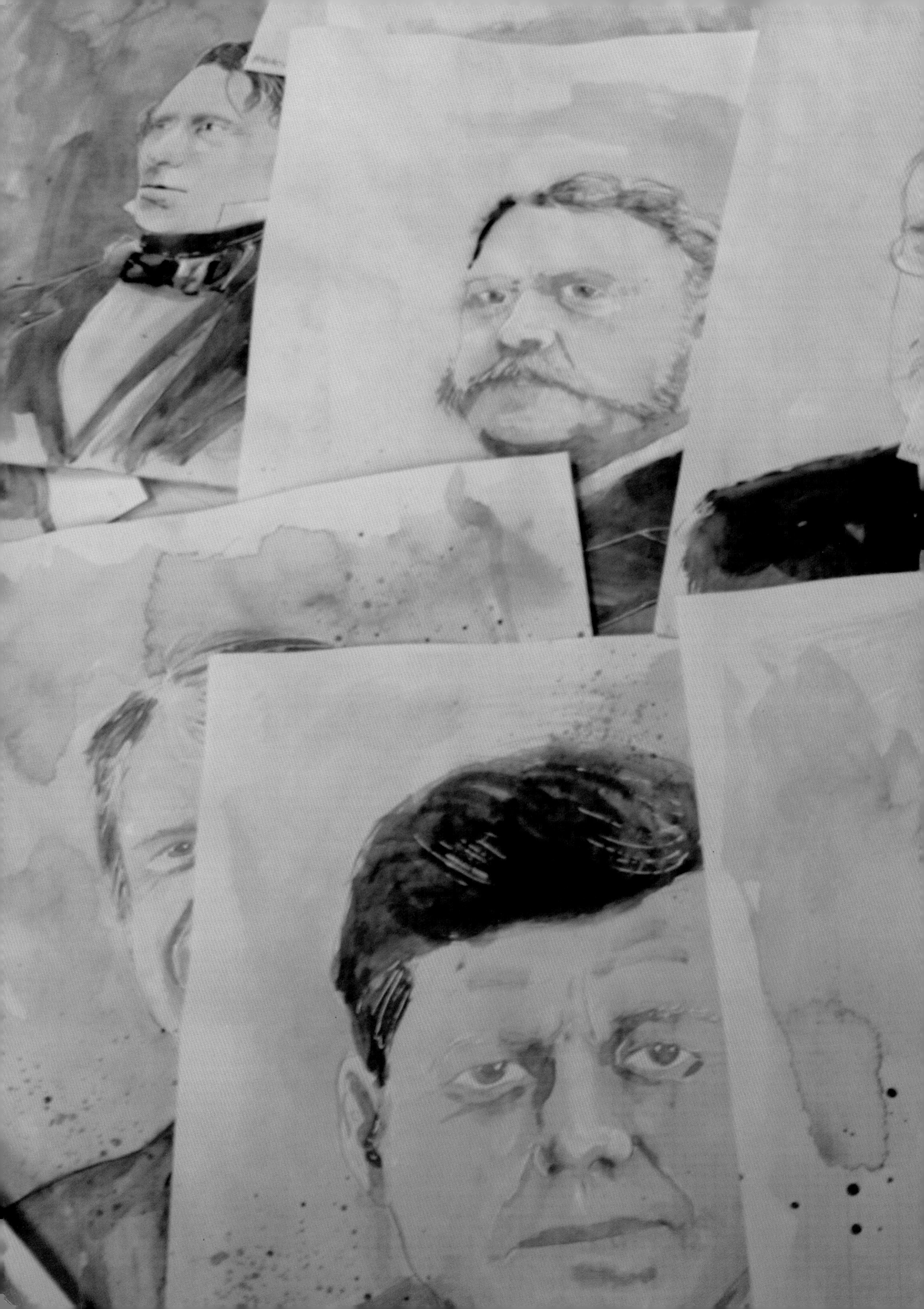

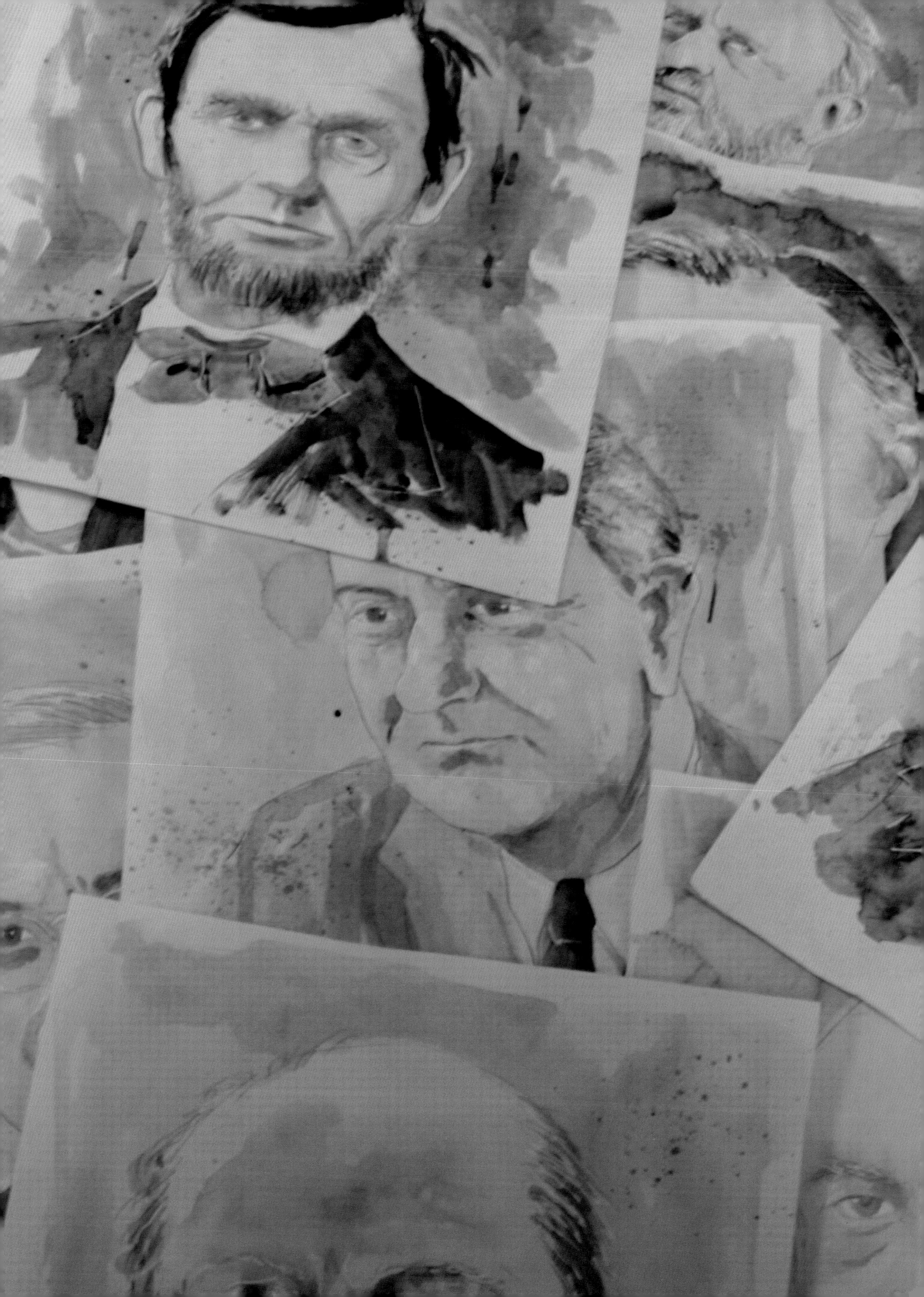

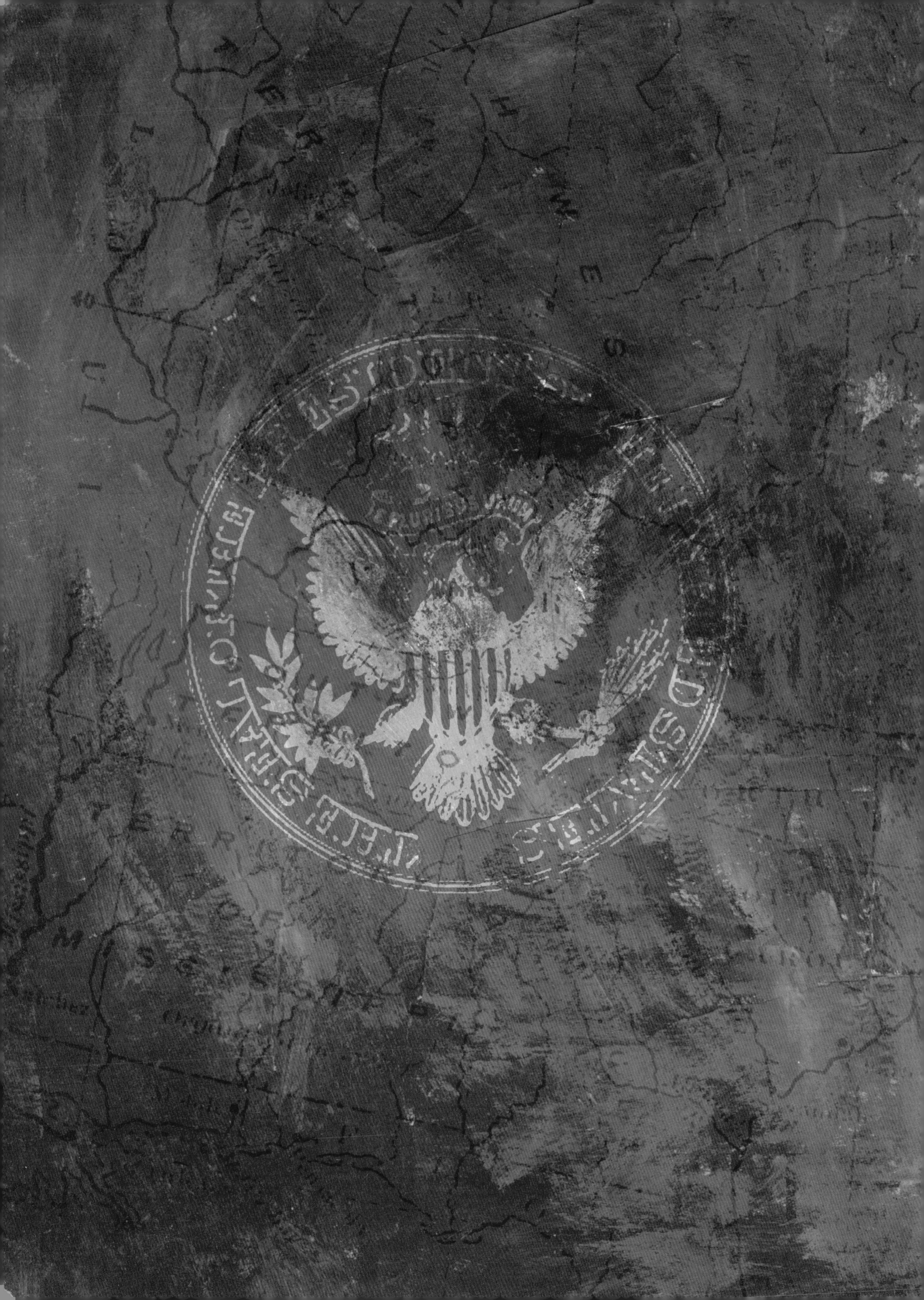